Library of Congress

CLASSIFICATION OUTLINE

Seventh Edition

LIBRARY OF CONGRESS

Library of Congress Cataloging-in-Publication Data

Library of Congress. Cataloging Policy and Support Office
    LC classification outline / prepared by the Library of Congress, Cataloging Policy and Support Office.—7th ed.
       p. cm.
    Rev. ed. of: LC classification outline / Office for Subject Cataloging Policy, Collections Services, Library of Congress, 6th ed. 1990.
    ISBN 0-8444-1100-0
    1. Classification, Library of Congress. 2. Classification—Books. I. Title: Library of Congress classification outline. II. Library of Congress. Office for Subject Cataloging Policy. LC classification outline. III. Title.

    Z696.U42 2003
    025.4'33—dc21

                        2003050786

For sale by the Library of Congress Cataloging Distribution Service, 101 Independence Avenue, S.E., Washington, DC 20541-4912. Product catalog available on the Web at <http://www.loc.gov/cds>.

Reprinted 2007 (with new Cover Design only)

CLASS A - GENERAL WORKS

Subclass AC

AC1-999	Collections. Series. Collected works
AC1-195	Collections of monographs, essays, etc.
AC1-8	American and English
AC9-195	Other languages
AC801-895	Inaugural and program dissertations
AC901-995	Pamphlet collections
AC999	Scrapbooks

Subclass AE

AE1-88	Encyclopedias
AE5-88	By language

Subclass AG

AG2-600	Dictionaries and other general reference works

Subclass AI

AI1-21	Indexes

Subclass AM

AM1-401	Museums. Collectors and collecting
AM10-100	By country
AM111-160	Museology. Museum methods, technique, etc.
AM200-401	Collectors and collecting

Subclass AN

AN	Newspapers
	For history and description of individual newspapers, see PN4891+

Subclass AP

AP1-230	Periodicals
AP101-115	Humorous periodicals
AP200-230	Juvenile periodicals

Subclass AS

AS1-945	Academies and learned societies
AS2.5-4	International associations, congresses, conferences, etc.
AS11-785	By region or country

Subclass AY

AY10-2001	Yearbooks. Almanacs. Directories
AY10-29	Annuals
AY30-1730	Almanacs
AY2001	Directories. General works on the compilation of directories, etc.
	Class directories by subject in B-Z

Subclass AZ

AZ101-999	History of scholarship and learning. The humanities
AZ101-111	Philosophy. Theory
AZ191-193	Evaluation
AZ200-361	History
AZ501-908	By region or country

CLASS B - PHILOSOPHY. PSYCHOLOGY. RELIGION

Subclass B

B1-5802	Philosophy (General)
B69-99	General works
B108-5802	By period
	Including individual philosophers and schools of philosophy
B108-708	Ancient
B720-765	Medieval
B770-785	Renaissance
B790-5802	Modern
B808-849	Special topics and schools of philosophy
B850-5739	By region or country
B5800-5802	By religion

Subclass BC

BC1-199	Logic
BC11-39	History
BC60-99	General works
BC171-199	Special topics

Subclass BD

BD10-701	Speculative philosophy
BD10-41	General philosophical works
BD95-131	Metaphysics
BD143-237	Epistemology. Theory of knowledge
BD240-260	Methodology
BD300-450	Ontology
	Including being, the soul, life, death
BD493-701	Cosmology
	Including teleology, space and time, structure of matter, plurality of worlds

Subclass BF

BF1-990	Psychology
BF38-64	Philosophy. Relation to other topics
BF173-175.5	Psychoanalysis
BF176-176.5	Psychological tests and testing
BF180-198.7	Experimental psychology
BF203	Gestalt psychology
BF207-209	Psychotropic drugs and other substances
BF231-299	Sensation. Aesthesiology
BF309-499	Consciousness. Cognition
	Including learning, attention, comprehension, memory, imagination, genius, intelligence, thought and thinking, psycholinguistics, mental fatigue

	Psychology - Continued
BF501-505	Motivation
BF511-593	Affection. Feeling. Emotion
BF608-635	Will. Volition. Choice. Control
BF636-637	Applied psychology
BF638-648	New Thought. Menticulture, etc.
BF660-685	Comparative psychology. Animal and human psychology
BF692-692.5	Psychology of sex. Sexual behavior
BF697-697.5	Differential psychology. Individuality. Self
BF698-698.9	Personality
BF699-711	Genetic psychology
BF712-724.85	Developmental psychology

Including infant psychology, child psychology, adolescence, adulthood

BF725-727	Class psychology
BF795-839	Temperament. Character
BF839.8-885	Physiognomy. Phrenology
BF889-905	Graphology. Study of handwriting
BF908-940	The hand. Palmistry
BF1001-1389	Parapsychology
BF1001-1045	Psychic research. Psychology of the conscious
BF1048-1108	Hallucinations. Sleep. Dreaming. Visions
BF1111-1156	Hypnotism. Suggestion. Mesmerism. Subliminal projection
BF1161-1171	Telepathy. Mind reading. Thought transference
BF1228-1389	Spiritualism

Including mediumship, spirit messages, clairvoyance

BF1404-2055	Occult sciences
BF1444-1486	Ghosts. Apparitions. Hauntings
BF1501-1562	Demonology. Satanism. Possession
BF1562.5-1584	Witchcraft
BF1585-1623	Magic. Hermetics. Necromancy
BF1651-1729	Astrology
BF1745-1779	Oracles. Sibyls. Divinations
BF1783-1815	Seers. Prophets. Prophecies
BF1845-1891	Fortune-telling
BF2050-2055	Human-alien encounters. Contact between humans and extraterrestrials

Subclass BH

BH1-301	Aesthetics
BH81-208	History
BH301	Special topics

Subclass BJ

BJ1-1725	Ethics
BJ71-1185	History and general works

Including individual ethical philosophers

BJ1188-1295	Religious ethics
BJ1298-1335	Evolutionary and genetic ethics

	Ethics - Continued
BJ1365-1385	Positivist ethics
BJ1388	Socialist ethics
BJ1390-1390.5	Communist ethics
BJ1392	Totalitarian ethics
BJ1395	Feminist ethics
BJ1518-1697	Individual ethics. Character. Virtue
	Including practical and applied ethics, conduct of life, vices, success, ethics for children
BJ1725	Ethics of social groups, classes, etc. Professional ethics
BJ1801-2195	Social usages. Etiquette
BJ2021-2078	Etiquette of entertaining
BJ2139-2156	Etiquette of travel
BJ2195	Telephone etiquette

Subclass BL

BL1-2790	Religions. Mythology. Rationalism
BL1-50	Religion (General)
BL51-65	Philosophy of religion. Psychology of religion. Religion in relation to other subjects
BL70-71	Sacred books (General)
BL71.5-73	Biography
BL74-99	Religions of the world
BL175-265	Natural theology
BL175-190	General
BL200	Theism
BL205-216	Nature and attributes of Deity
BL217	Polytheism
BL218	Dualism
BL220	Pantheism
BL221	Monotheism
BL224-227	Creation. Theory of the earth
BL239-265	Religion and science
BL270	Unity and plurality
BL290	The soul
BL300-325	The myth. Comparative mythology
BL350-385	Classification of religions
BL410	Religions in relation to one another
BL425-490	Religious doctrines (General)
BL430	Origins of religion
BL435-457	Nature worship
BL458	Women in comparative religion
BL460	Sex worship. Phallicism
BL465-470	Worship of human beings
BL473-490	Other
BL500-547	Eschatology
BL550-619	Worship. Cultus
BL624-629.5	Religious life
BL630-632	Religious organization

BL660-2680	History and principles of religions
BL660	Indo-European. Aryan
BL685	Ural-Altaic
BL687	Mediterranean region
BL689-980	European. Occidental
BL700-820	Classical (Etruscan, Greek, Roman)
BL830-875	Germanic and Norse
BL900-980	Other European
BL1000-2370	Asian. Oriental
BL1050-1060	By region
BL1100-1295	Hinduism
BL1100-1107.5	General
BL1108.2-1108.7	Religious education
BL1109.2-1109.7	Antiquities. Archaeology. Inscriptions
BL1111-1143.2	Sacred books. Sources
BL1145-1146	Hindu literature
BL1153.7-1168	By region or country
BL1212.32-1215	Doctrines. Theology
BL1216-1225	Hindu pantheon. Deities
BL1225.2-1243.58	Religious life
BL1243.72-1243.78	Monasteries. Temples, etc.
BL1271.2-1295	Modifications. Sects
BL1284.5-1289.592	Vaishnavism
BL1300-1380	Jainism
BL1310-1314.2	Sacred books. Sources
BL1315-1317	Jain literature
BL1375.3-1375.7	Jaina pantheon. Deities
BL1376-1378.85	Forms of worship
BL1379-1380	Modifications, etc.
BL1500-1590	Zoroastrianism (Mazdeism). Parseeism
BL1595	Yezidis
BL1600-1695	Semitic religions
BL1600-1605	General
BL1610	Aramean
BL1615-1616	Sumerian
BL1620-1625	Assyro-Babylonian
BL1630	Chaldean
BL1635	Harranian. Pseudo-Sabian
BL1640-1645	Syrian. Palestinian. Samaritan
BL1650	Hebrew
	For Judaism, see subclass BM
BL1660-1665	Phoenician. Carthaginian, etc.
BL1670-1672	Canaanite
BL1675	Moabite. Philistine
BL1680-1685	Arabian (except Islam)
BL1695	Druses
BL1710	Ethiopian
BL1750-2350	By region or country
BL1790-1975	China
BL1830-1883	Confucianism
BL1899-1942.85	Taoism

Subclass BM

Subclass BP

	Islam. Bahai Faith. Theosophy, etc.
	Islam - Continued
BP166-166.94	Theology (Kalām)
BP167.5	Heresy, heresies, heretics
BP168	Apostasy from Islam
BP169	Works against Islam and the Koran
BP170	Works in defense of Islam. Islamic apologetics
BP170.2	Benevolent work. Social work. Welfare work, etc.
BP170.3-170.5	Missionary work of Islam
BP171-173	Relation of Islam to other religions
BP173.25-173.45	Islamic sociology
BP174-190	The practice of Islam
BP176-181	The five duties of a Moslem. Pillars of Islam
BP182	Jihad (Holy War)
BP184-184.9	Religious ceremonies, rites, etc.
BP186-186.97	Special days and seasons, fasts, feasts, festivals, etc. Relics
BP187-187.9	Shrines, sacred places, etc.
BP188-190	Islamic religious life
BP188.2-188.3	Devotional literature
BP188.45-189.65	Sufism. Mysticism. Dervishes
BP189.68-189.7	Monasticism
BP191-253	Branches, sects, etc.
BP300-395	Bahai Faith
BP500-585	Theosophy
BP595-597	Anthroposophy
BP600-610	Other beliefs and movements

Subclass BQ

BQ1-9800	Buddhism
BQ251-799	History
BQ800-829	Persecutions
BQ840-999	Biography
BQ860-999	Individual
BQ860-939	Gautama Buddha
BQ1001-1045	Buddhist literature
BQ1100-3340	Tripiṭaka (Canonical literature)
BQ4000-4060	General works
BQ4061-4570	Doctrinal and systematic Buddhism
BQ4600-4610	Relation to other religious and philosophical systems
BQ4620-4905	Buddhist pantheon
BQ4911-5720	Practice of Buddhism. Forms of worship
BQ4965-5030	Ceremonies and rites. Ceremonial rules
BQ5035-5065	Hymns. Chants. Recitations
BQ5070-5075	Altar, liturgical objects, ornaments, memorials, etc.
BQ5080-5085	Vestments, altar cloths, etc.
BQ5090-5095	Liturgical functions
BQ5100-5125	Symbols and symbolism
BQ5130-5137	Temple. Temple organization
BQ5140-5355	Buddhist ministry. Priesthood. Organization
BQ5360-5680	Religious life

Buddhism

Practice of Buddhism. Forms of worship - Continued

BQ5700-5720	Festivals. Days and seasons
BQ5725-5845	Folklore
BQ5851-5899	Benevolent work. Social work. Welfare work, etc.
BQ5901-5975	Missionary work
BQ6001-6160	Monasticism and monastic life Saṃgha (Order)
BQ6200-6240	Asceticism. Hermits. Wayfaring life
BQ6300-6388	Monasteries. Temples. Shrines. Sites
BQ6400-6495	Pilgrims and pilgrimages
BQ7001-9800	Modifications, schools, etc.
BQ7100-7285	Theravāda (Hinayana) Buddhism
BQ7300-7529	Mahayana Buddhism
BQ7530-7950	Tibetan Buddhism (Lamaism)
BQ7960-7989	Bonpo (Sect)
BQ8000-9800	Special modifications, sects, etc.
BQ8500-8769	Pure Land Buddhism
BQ8900-9099	Tantric Buddhism
BQ9250-9519	Zen Buddhism

Subclass BR

BR1-1725	Christianity
BR60-67	Early Christian literature. Fathers of the Church, etc.
BR140-1510	History
BR160-481	By period
BR500-1510	By region or country
BR1690-1725	Biography

Subclass BS

BS1-2970	The Bible
BS11-115	Early versions
BS125-355	Modern texts and versions
BS410-680	Works about the Bible
BS701-1830	Old Testament
BS1901-2970	New Testament
BS2280-2545	Works about the New Testament
BS2547-2970	Special parts of the New Testament

Subclass BT

BT10-1480	Doctrinal Theology
BT19-37	Doctrine and dogma
BT93-93.6	Judaism
BT95-97.2	Divine law. Moral government
BT98-180	God
BT198-590	Christology
BT595-680	Mary, Mother of Jesus Christ. Mariology
BT695-749	Creation
BT750-811	Salvation. Soteriology

BT819-891	Eschatology. Last things
BT899-940	Future state. Future life
BT960-985	Invisible world (saints, demons, etc.)
BT990-1010	Creeds, confessions, covenants, etc.
BT1029-1040	Catechisms
BT1095-1255	Apologetics. Evidences of Christianity
BT1313-1480	History of specific doctrines and movements. Heresies and schisms

Subclass BV

BV1-5099	Practical Theology
BV5-530	Worship (Public and private)
BV30-135	Times and seasons. The Church year
BV150-168	Christian symbols and symbolism
BV169-199	Liturgy and ritual
BV200	Family worship
BV205-287	Prayer
BV301-530	Hymnology
BV590-1652	Ecclesiastical theology
BV659-683	Ministry. Clergy. Religious vocations
BV700-707	Parish. Congregation. The local church
BV800-873	Sacraments. Ordinances
BV895-896	Shrines. Holy places
BV900-1450	Religious societies, associations, etc.
BV1460-1615	Religious education (General)
BV1620-1652	Social life, recreation, etc., in the church
BV2000-3705	Missions
BV2123-2595	Special churches
BV2610-2695	Special types of missions
BV2750-3695	Missions in individual countries
BV3750-3799	Evangelism. Revivals
BV4000-4470	Pastoral theology
BV4485-5099	Practical religion. The Christian life

Subclass BX

BX1-9999	Christian Denominations
BX1-9.5	Church unity. Ecumenical movement. Interdenominational cooperation
BX100-189	Eastern churches. Oriental churches
BX200-756	Orthodox Eastern Church
BX800-4795	Catholic Church
BX2400-4563	Monasticism. Religious orders
BX4600-4644	Churches, cathedrals, abbeys (as parish churches), etc.
BX4650-4705	Biography and portraits
BX4710.1-4715.95	Eastern churches in communion with Rome. Catholics of the Oriental rites. Uniats
BX4716.4-4795	Dissenting sects other than Protestant

BX4800-9999	Protestantism
BX4872-4924	Pre-Reformation
BX4929-4951	Post-Reformation
BX5001-5009	Anglican Communion (General)
BX5011-5207	Church of England
BX5210-5395	Episcopal Church in Scotland
BX5410-5595	Church of Ireland
BX5596-5598	Church in Wales
BX5600-5740	Church of England outside of Great Britain
BX5601-5620	Anglican Church of Canada
BX5800-5995	Protestant Episcopal Church in the United States of America
BX5996-6030	Protestant Episcopal Church outside the United States
BX6051-6093	Reformed Episcopal Church
BX6101-9999	Other Protestant denominations
	Alphabetical; only larger denominations listed
	The subarrangement is essentially the same for each sect, the primary features being indicated by way of example under Baptists
BX6101-6193	Adventists. "Millerites"
BX6195-6197	Arminians. Remonstrants
BX6201-6495	Baptists
BX6201-6227	General
BX6231-6328	History. Local divisions
BX6329	Baptists and other churches
BX6330-6331.2	Doctrine
BX6333	Sermons. Tracts
BX6334	Controversial works
BX6335-6336	Creeds. Catechisms
BX6337	Service. Ritual. Liturgy
BX6338-6339	Sacraments
BX6340-6346.3	Government. Discipline
BX6349-6470	Individual branches
BX6480-6490	Individual Baptist churches
BX6493-6495	Biography
BX6551-6593	Catholic Apostolic Church. Irvingites
BX6651-6693	Christadelphians. Brothers of Christ
BX6751-6793	Christian Church
	See also Disciples of Christ
BX6801-6843	Christian Reformed Church
BX6901-6997	Christian Science
BX7003	Christian Union
BX7020-7060	Church of God
BX7079-7097	Churches of God
BX7101-7260	Congregationalism
BX7301-7343	Disciples of Christ. Campbellites
BX7401-7430	Dowieism. Christian Catholic Church
BX7451-7493	Evangelical and Reformed Church
BX7556	Evangelical United Brethren Church
BX7580-7583	Free Congregations (Germany). Freie Gemeinden
BX7601-7795	Friends. Society of Friends. Quakers
BX7801-7843	German Baptist Brethren. Church of the Brethren. Dunkards

Protestantism

Other Protestant denominations - Continued

BX7850-7865	German Evangelical Protestant Church of North America. Evangelical Protestant Church of North America
BX7901-7943	German Evangelical Synod of North America
BX7990.H6-.H69	Holiness churches
BX8001-8080	Lutheran churches
BX8101-8144	Mennonites
BX8201-8495	Methodism
BX8525-8528	Millennial Dawnists. Jehovah's Witnesses
BX8551-8593	Moravian Church. United Brethren. Unitas Fratrum. Herrnhuters
BX8601-8695	Mormons. Church of Jesus Christ of Latter-Day Saints
BX8701-8749	New Jerusalem Church. New Church. Swedenborgianism
BX8762-8785	Pentecostal churches
BX8799-8809	Plymouth Brethren. Darbyites
BX8901-9225	Presbyterianism. Calvinistic Methodism
BX9301-9359	Puritanism
BX9401-9640	Reformed or Calvinistic Churches
BX9675	River Brethren. Brethren in Christ
BX9701-9743	Salvation Army
BX9751-9793	Shakers. United Society of Believers. Millennial Church
BX9801-9869	Unitarianism
BX9875-9877.1	United Brethren in Christ. Church of the United Brethren in Christ
BX9881-9882.95	United Church of Canada
BX9884-9886	United Church of Christ
BX9887	United Evangelical Church
BX9889	United Missionary Church
BX9901-9969	Unviersalism. Universalists
BX9975	Volunteers of America
BX9980	Walloon Church
BX9998	Other beliefs and movements akin to Christianity
BX9999	Independent churches, parishes, societies, etc.

CLASS C - AUXILIARY SCIENCES OF HISTORY

Subclass C

C1-51   Auxiliary Sciences of History (General)

Subclass CB

CB3-482	History of Civilization
CB156	Terrestrial evidence of interplanetary voyages
CB158-161	Forecasts of future progress
CB195-281	Civilization and race
CB305-430	By period
CB440-482	Relation to special topics

Subclass CC

CC1-960	Archaeology
CC72-81	Philosophy. Theory
CC83-97	Study and teaching. Research
CC135-137	Preservation, restoration, and conservation of antiquities. Antiquities and state
CC140	Forgeries of antiquities
CC200-260	Bells. Campanology. Cowbells
CC300-350	Crosses
CC600-605	Boundary stones
CC700-705	Stone heaps, cairns, etc., of unknown purpose

Subclass CD

CD1-6471	Diplomatics. Archives. Seals
CD1-511	Diplomatics
CD921-4280	Archives
CD5001-6471	Seals

Subclass CE

CE1-97	Technical Chronology. Calendar
CE21-46	Ancient
CE51-85	Medieval and modern
CE91-92	Perpetual calendars. Century calendars, etc.

Subclass CJ

CJ1-6661	Numismatics
CJ1-4625	Coins
CJ4801-5450	Tokens
CJ5501-6661	Medals and medallions

Subclass CN

CN1-1355	Inscriptions. Epigraphy
CN120-740	Ancient inscriptions
CN750-753	Early Christian inscriptions
CN755	Medieval inscriptions (General)
CN760	Modern inscriptions (General)
CN805-865	By language
CN870-1355	By region or country

Subclass CR

CR1-6305	Heraldry
CR51-79	Crests, monograms, devices, badges, mottoes, etc.
CR91-93	Shields and supporters
CR101-115	Flags, banners, and standards
CR191-1020	Public and official heraldry
CR1101-1131	Ecclesiastical and sacred heraldry
CR1179-3395	Family heraldry
CR3499-4420	Titles of honor, rank, precedence, etc.
CR4480-4485	Royalty. Insignia. Regalia, crown and coronets, etc.
CR4501-6305	Chivalry and knighthood (Orders, decorations, etc.)
CR4547-4553	Ceremonials, pageants, tournaments, etc.
CR4571-4595	Duels and dueling
CR4651-6305	Orders, etc.

Subclass CS

CS1-3090	Genealogy
CS23-35	Genealogical lists, etc., covering more than one country or continent
CS38-39	Family history covering more than one country
CS42-2209	By region or country
CS2300-3090	Personal and family names

Subclass CT

CT21-9999	Biography
CT21-22	Biography as an art or literary form
CT31-83	History of biographical literature. Lives of biographers
CT93-206	General collective biography
CT210-3150	National biography
CT3200-9999	Biography. By subject
CT3200-3830	Biography of women (Collective)
CT3990	Academicians. Scholars. Savants
CT9960-9998	Other miscellaneous groups
CT9999	Blank books for personal records, diaries, etc.

CLASS D - HISTORY (GENERAL) AND HISTORY OF EUROPE

Subclass D

D1-2009	History (General)
D1-24.5	General
D25-27	Military and naval history
D31-34	Political and diplomatic history
D51-90	Ancient history
D101-110.5	Medieval and modern history, 476-
D111-203	Medieval history
D205-472	Modern history, 1453-
D219-234	1453-1648
D242-283.5	1601-1715. 17th century
D284-297	1715-1789. 18th century
D299-472	1789-
D301-309	Period of the French Revolution
D351-400	19th century. 1801-1914/1920
D410-472	20th century
D501-680	World War I (1914-1918)
D720-728	Period between World Wars (1919-1939)
D731-838	World War II (1939-1945)
D839-860	Post-war history (1945-)
D880-888	Developing countries
D890-893	Eastern Hemisphere
D900-2009	Europe (General)
D901-980	Description and travel
D1050-2009	History

Subclass DA

DA1-995	History of Great Britain
DA10-18.2	British Empire. Commonwealth of Nations. The Commonwealth
DA20-690	England
DA28-592	History
DA129-592	By period
DA129-260	Early and medieval to 1485
DA300-592	Modern, 1485-
DA600-667	Description and travel. Guidebooks
DA670-690	Local history and description
DA700-745	Wales
DA750-890	Scotland
DA900-995	Ireland
DA990.U45-U46	Northern Ireland (Ulster)

Subclass DAW

DAW1001-1051	History of Central Europe

Subclass DB

DB1-3150	History of Austria. Liechtenstein. Hungary. Czechoslovakia
DB1-879	Austria. Austro-Hungarian Empire
DB881-898	Liechtenstein
DB901-999	Hungary
DB2000-3150	Czechoslovakia
DB2300-2650	Local history and description of Czech lands
DB2700-3150	Slovakia

Subclass DC

DC1-947	History of France
DC35-424	History
DC60-424	By period
DC60-109	Early and medieval to 1515
DC110-424	Modern, 1515-
DC139-249	Revolutionary and Napoleonic period, 1789-1815
DC251-354.9	19th century
DC361-424	20th century
DC600-801	Local history and description
DC921-930	Andorra
DC941-947	Monaco

Subclass DD

DD1-901	History of Germany
DD84-257.4	History
DD121-257.4	By period
DD121-124	Earliest to 481
DD125-174.6	Early and medieval to 1519
DD175-257.4	Modern, 1519-
DD258-262	West Germany
DD280-289.5	East Germany
DD301-454	Prussia
DD701-901	Local history and description

Subclass DE

DE1-100	History of the Greco-Roman world

Subclass DF

DF10-951	History of Greece
DF10-289	Ancient Greece
DF501-649	Medieval Greece. Byzantine Empire, 323-1453
DF701-951	Modern Greece
DF895-951	Local history and description

Subclass DG

DG11-999	History of Italy
DG11-365	Ancient Italy. Rome to 476
DG401-583.8	Medieval and modern Italy, 476-
DG600-684.72	Northern Italy
DG691-817.3	Central Italy
DG819-875	Southern Italy
DG975	Other cities (non-metropolitan), provinces, etc., A-Z
DG987-999	Malta. Maltese Islands

Subclass DH

DH1-925	History of Low Countries. Benelux Countries
DH95-207	History
DH141-207	By period
DH401-811	Belgium
DH503-694	History
DH571-694	By period
DH571-584	Early and medieval to 1555
DH585-619	1555-1794. Spanish and Austrian rule
DH620-676	1794-1909
DH677-694	20th century
DH801-811	Local history and description
DH901-925	Luxembourg

Subclass DJ

DJ1-411	History of Netherlands (Holland)
DJ95-292	History
DJ151-292	By period
DJ151-152	Early and medieval to 1555
DJ154-210	1555-1795. United provinces
DJ211	1795-1806. Batavian Republic
DJ215-292	19th-20th centuries
DJ401-411	Local history and description

Subclass DJK

DJK1-77	History of Eastern Europe (General)
DJK26-28	Ethnography
DJK27	Slavic peoples (General)
DJK30-51	History
DJK61-77	Local history and description
DJK61-66	Black Sea region
DJK71-76	Carpathian Mountain Region
DJK76.2-76.8	Danube River Valley
DJK77	Pannonia

Subclass DK

DK1-949.5	History of Russia. Soviet Union. Former Soviet Republics
DK36-293	History
DK70-112.42	Early to 1613
DK70-99.7	Rus'
DK99.8-112.42	Muscovy
DK112.8-264.8	House of Romanov, 1613-1917
DK265-265.95	Revolution, 1917-1921
DK266-292	Soviet regime, 1918-1991
DK293	1991-
DK500	Regions not limited to one Republic, A-Z
DK501-949.5	Local history and description
DK502.3-502.75	Baltic States
DK503-503.95	Estonia
DK504-504.95	Latvia
DK505-505.95	Lithuania
DK507-507.95	Belarus. Byelorussian S.S.R. White Russia
DK508-508.95	Ukraine
DK509	Southern Soviet Union
DK509.1-509.95	Moldova. Moldovian S.S.R. Bessarabia
DK510-651	Russia (Federation). Russian S.F.S.R.
DK670-679.5	Georgia (Republic). Georgian S.S.R. Georgian Sakartvelo
DK680-689.5	Armenia (Republic). Armenian S.S.R.
DK690-699.5	Azerbaijan. Azerbaijan S.S.R.
DK751-781	Siberia
DK845-860	Soviet Central Asia. West Turkestan
DK901-909.5	Kazakhstan. Kazakh S.S.R.
DK911-919.5	Kyrgyzstan. Kirghiz S.S.R. Kirghizia
DK921-929.5	Tajikistan. Tajik S.S.R. Tadzhikistan
DK931-939.5	Turkmenistan. Turkmen S.S.R. Turkmenia
DK941-949.5	Uzbekistan. Uzbek S.S.R.
DK4010-4800	History of Poland
DK4123-4452	History
DK4186-4348	To 1795
DK4348.5-4395	1795-1918. 19th century (General)
DK4397-4420	1918-1945
DK4429-4442	1945-1989. People's Republic
DK4445-4452	1989-
DK4600-4800	Local history and description

Subclass DL

DL1-1180	History of Northern Europe. Scandinavia
DL43-87	History
DL61-87	By period
DL101-291	Denmark
DL143-263.3	History
DL160-263.3	By period
DL160-183.9	Early and medieval to 1523
DL184-263.3	Modern, 1523-

DL301-398	Iceland
DL401-596	Norway
DL443-537	History
DL460-537	By period
DL460-478	Early and medieval to 1387
DL480-502	1387-1814. Union of Kalmar, 1397
DL503-526	1814-1905. 19th century
DL527-537	20th century. Period of World War II, 1939-1945
DL576-596	Local history and description
DL601-991	Sweden
DL643-879	History
DL660-879	By period
DL660-700.9	Early and medieval to 1523. Union of Kalmar, 1397
DL701-879	Modern, 1523-
DL971-991	Local history and description
DL1002-1180	Finland
DL1024-1141.6	History
DL1050-1141.6	By period
DL1050-1052.9	Early to 1523
DL1055-1141.6	Modern, 1523-
DL1070-1078	Revolution, 1917-1918. Civil War
DL1090-1105	1939-1945
DL1095-1105	Russo-Finnish War, 1939-1940
DL1170-1180	Local history and description

Subclass DP

DP1-402	History of Spain
DP56-272.4	History
DP91-272.4	By period
DP91-96	Earliest to 711
DP97.3-160.8	711-1516. Moorish domination and the Reconquest
DP161-272.4	Modern Spain, 1479/1516-
DP161.5-166	1479-1516. Fernando V and Isabel I
DP170-189	1516-1700. Habsburgs
DP192-200.8	1700-1808. Bourbons
DP201-232.6	1808-1886. 19th century
DP233-272.4	20th century. 1886-
DP285-402	Local history and description
DP501-900	History of Portugal
DP535-682.2	History
DP558-682.2	By period
DP558-618	Early and medieval to 1580
DP620-682.2	1580-
DP702-802	Local history and description

Subclass DQ

DQ1-851	History of Switzerland
DQ51-210	History

	History of Switzerland
	History - Continued
DQ78-210	By period
DQ78-110	Early and medieval to 1516
DQ111-123	1516-1798
DQ124-191	19th century
DQ201-210	20th century
DQ301-851	Local history and description

Subclass DR

DR1-2285	History of Balkan Peninsula
DR32-48.5	History. Balkan War, 1912-1913
DR50-50.84	Thrace
DR51-98	Bulgaria
DR65-93.47	History
DR73.7-93.47	By period
DR73.7-80.8	Early and medieval
DR81-84	Turkish rule, 1396-1878
DR84.9-89.8	1878-1944
DR89.9-93.34	1944-1990
DR93.4-93.47	1990-
DR95-98	Local history and description
DR201-296	Romania
DR215-269.6	History
DR238-269.6	By period
DR238-240.5	Early and medieval to 1601. Roman period
DR241-241.5	Phanariote regime, 1601-1822
DR242-249	1822-1881. 19th century
DR250-266.5	1866/1881-1944
DR267-267.5	1944-1989
DR268-269.6	1989-
DR279-296	Local history and description
DR401-741	Turkey
DR436-605	History
DR481-605	By period
DR481	Earliest to 1281/1453
DR485-555.7	1281/1453-1789. Fall of Constantinople, 1453
DR511-529	1566-1640. Period of decline
DR531-555.7	1640-1789
DR556-567	1789-1861. 19th century
DR568-575	1861-1909. War with Russia, 1877-1878
DR576-605	20th century. Constitutional movement
DR701-741	Local history and description (European Turkey)
DR901-998	Albania
DR927-978.52	History
DR954-978.52	By period
DR954-960.5	To 1501
DR961-969	1501-1912. Turkish rule
DR969.8-978.52	20th century
DR996-998	Local history and description

DR1202-2285	Yugoslavia
DR1232-1321	History
DR1259-1321	By period
DR1259-1265	Early and medieval to 1500
DR1266-1272	1500-1800
DR1273-1280	1800-1918
DR1281-1321	1918-
DR1313-1313.8	Yugoslav War, 1991-1995
DR1315-1321	1992-
DR1350-2285	Local history and description
DR1352-1485	Slovenia
DR1502-1645	Croatia
DR1652-1785	Bosnia and Hercegovina
DR1802-1928	Montenegro
DR1932-2125	Serbia
DR2152-2285	Macedonia

Subclass DS

DS1-937	History of Asia
DS5.95-10	Description and travel
DS11	Antiquities
DS13-28	Ethnography
DS31-35.2	History
DS35.3-35.77	The Islamic World
DS36-39.2	Arab countries
DS36.9	Ethnography
DS37-39.2	History
DS41-66	Middle East. Southwestern Asia. Ancient Orient. Arab East. Near East
DS51-54.95	Local history and description
DS54-54.95	Cyprus
DS67-79.9	Iraq (Assyria, Babylonia, Mesopotamia)
DS80-90	Lebanon (Phenicia)
DS92-99	Syria
DS101-151	Israel (Palestine). The Jews
DS133-151	Jews outside of Palestine
DS153-154.9	Jordan. Transjordan
DS155-156	Asia Minor
DS161-195.5	Armenia
DS201-248	Arabian Peninsula. Saudi Arabia
DS251-326	Iran (Persia)
DS327-329.4	Central Asia
DS331-349.9	Southern Asia. Indian Ocean Region
DS349.8-349.9	Islands of the Indian Ocean
DS350-375	Afghanistan
DS376-392.2	Pakistan
DS393-396.9	Bangladesh. East Pakistan
DS401-486.5	India (Bharat)
DS488-490	Sri Lanka

DS491-492.9	Bhutan
DS493-495.8	Nepal
DS498-498.8	Goa. Portuguese in India
DS501-518.9	East Asia. The Far East
DS520-560.72	Southeastern Asia
DS524-526.7	History
DS527-530.9	Burma
DS531-560.72	French Indochina
DS541-553.7	History
DS554-554.98	Cambodia
DS555-555.98	Laos
DS556-559.93	Vietnam. Annam
DS560-560.72	Democratic Republic (North Vietnam), 1945-
DS561-589	Thailand (Siam)
DS591-599	Malaysia. Malay Peninsula. Straits Settlements
DS597.33-597.34	Sabah. British North Borneo
DS597.36-597.39	Sarawak
DS600-605	Malay Archipelago
DS608-610.9	Singapore
DS611-649	Indonesia (Dutch East Indies)
DS631-632	Ethnography
DS633-644.46	History
DS646.1-646.15	Sumatra
DS646.17-646.29	Java
DS646.3-646.34	Borneo. Kalimantan, Indonesia
DS646.4-646.49	Celebes. Sulawesi
DS646.5-646.59	Timor
DS646.6-646.69	Moluccas. Maluku
DS650-650.99	Brunei
DS651-689	Philippines
DS701-799.9	China
DS730-731	Ethnography
DS733-779.32	History
DS781-796	Local history and description
DS781-784.2	Manchuria
DS785-786	Tibet
DS796.H7	Hong Kong
DS798	Outer Mongolia. Mongolian People's Republic
DS798.92-799.9	Taiwan
DS801-897	Japan
DS833-891.5	History
DS894.215-897	Local history and description
DS901-937	Korea
DS904.8-922.4642	History
DS918-921.8	War and intervention, 1950-1953
DS924-925	Local history and description
DS930-937	Democratic People's Republic, 1948-

Subclass DT

DT1-3415	History of Africa
DT7-12.25	Description and travel
DT15-16	Ethnography
DT17-39	History
DT43-154	Egypt
DT56.8-69.5	Antiquities
DT63-63.5	Pyramids
DT68-68.8	Religious antiquities
DT74-107.87	History
DT115-154	Local history and description
DT139-153.5	Cairo
DT154.1-159.9	Sudan. Anglo-Egyptian Sudan
DT160-177	North Africa
DT167-176	History
DT168-169.5	Carthaginian period
DT179.2-179.9	Northwest Africa
DT181-346	Maghrib. Barbery States
DT211-239	Libya
DT241-269	Tunisia (Tunis)
DT271-299	Algeria
DT301-330	Morocco
DT330	Spanish Morocco
DT331-346	Sahara
DT348-363.3	Central Sub-Saharan Africa
DT365-469	Eastern Africa
DT367-367.8	Northeast Africa
DT371-390	Ethiopia (Abyssinia)
DT391-398	Eritrea
DT401-409	Somalia. Somaliland and adjacent territory
DT411-411.9	Djibouti. French Territory of the Afars and Issas. French Somaliland
DT421-432.5	East Africa. British East Africa
DT433.2-433.29	Uganda
DT433.5-434	Kenya
DT436-449	Tanzania. Tanganyika. German East Africa
DT449.Z2	Zanzibar
DT450-450.49	Rwanda. Ruanda-Urundi
DT450.5-450.95	Burundi
DT468-469	Islands (East African coast)
DT469.M21-.M38	Madagascar
DT469.M39	Mascarene Islands
DT469.M4-.M495	Mautitius (Ile de France)
DT469.M4975	Mayotte
DT469.R3-.R5	Reunion
DT469.S4-.S49	Seychelles
DT470-671	West Africa. West Coast
DT491-516.9	British West Africa
DT507	Ashanti Empire
DT509-509.9	Gambia
DT509.97-512.9	Ghana (Gold Coast)

History of Africa
    West Africa. West Coast
        British West Africa - Continued

DT515-515.9	Nigeria
DT516-516.9	Sierra Leone
DT521-555.9	French West Africa. French Sahara. West Sahara. Sahel
DT541-541.9	Benin. Dahomey
DT543-543.9	Guinea
DT545-545.9	Cote d'Ivoire. Ivory Coast
DT546.1-546.49	French-speaking Equatorial Africa
DT546.1-546.19	Gabon (Gaboon, Gabun)
DT546.2-546.29	Congo (Brazaville). Middle Congo
DT546.3-546.39	Central African Republic. Central African Empire. Ubangi-Shari
DT546.4-546.49	Chad (Tchad)
DT547-547.9	Niger
DT548	West Sahara
DT549-549.9	Senegal
DT551-551.9	Mali. Mali Federation. Sudanese Republic. French Sudan
DT554-554.9	Mauritania
DT555-555.9	Burkina Faso. Upper Volta
DT561-581	Cameroon (Cameroun, Kamerun)
DT582-582.9	Togo. Togoland
DT591-615.9	Portuguese-speaking West Africa
DT613-613.9	Guinea-Bissau. Portuguese Guinea
DT615-615.9	Sao Tome and Principe
DT619-620.9	Spanish West Africa
DT620-620.9	Equatorial Guinea (Spanish Guinea)
DT621-637	Liberia
DT639	Congo (Kongo) River region
DT641-665	Zaire. Congo (Democratic Republic). Belgian Congo
DT669-671	Islands
DT671.C2	Cape Verde
DT1001-1190	Southern Africa
DT1251-1465	Angola
DT1501-1685	Namibia. South-West Africa
DT1701-2405	South Africa
DT1772-1974	History
DT1991-2054	Cape Province. Cape of Good Hope
DT2075-2145	Orange Free State. Oranje Vrystaat
DT2181-2278	KwaZulu-Natal. Natal
DT2291-2378	Transvaal. South African Republic
DT2421-2525	Botswana. Bechuanaland
DT2541-2686	Lesotho. Basutoland
DT2701-2825	Swaziland
DT2831-2864	British Central Africa. Federation of Rhodesia and Nyasaland
DT2871-3025	Zimbabwe. Southern Rhodesia
DT3031-3145	Zambia. Northern Rhodesia
DT3161-3257	Malawi. Nyasaland
DT3291-3415	Mozambique

Subclass DU

DU1-950	History of Oceania (South Seas)
DU28.11-68	History
DU80-398	Australia
DU145	Australian Capital Territory. Canberra
DU150-180	New South Wales
DU182-198	Tasmania. Van Diemen's Land
DU200-230	Victoria
DU250-280	Queensland
DU300-330	South Australia
DU350-380	Western Australia
DU390	Central Australia
DU391	Northern Australia
DU392-398	Northern Territory of Australia
DU400-430	New Zealand
DU490	Melanesia (General)
DU500	Micronesia (General)
DU510	Polynesia (General)
DU520-950	Smaller Island Groups
DU620-629	Hawaiian Islands. Hawaii
DU739-747	New Guinea
DU810-819	Samoan Islands

Subclass DX

DX101-301	History of Gypsies

Class E

Class F

F106	Atlantic coast. Middle Atlantic States
F116-130	New York
F131-145	New Jersey
F146-160	Pennsylvania
F161-175	Delaware
F176-190	Maryland
F191-205	District of Columbia. Washington
F206-220	The South. South Atlantic States
F221-235	Virginia
F236-250	West Virginia
F251-265	North Carolina
F266-280	South Carolina
F281-295	Georgia
F296-301	Gulf States. West Florida
F306-320	Florida
F321-335	Alabama
F336-350	Mississippi
F350.5-355	Mississippi River and Valley. Middle West
F366-380	Louisiana
F381-395	Texas
F396	Old Southwest. Lower Mississippi Valley
F406-420	Arkansas
F431-445	Tennessee
F446-460	Kentucky
F461-475	Missouri
F476-485	Old Northwest. Northwest Territory
F486-500	Ohio
F516-520	Ohio River and Valley
F521-535	Indiana
F536-550	Illinois
F550.5-558.2	The Lake region. Great Lakes
F561-575	Michigan
F576-590	Wisconsin
F590.3-596.3	The West. Trans-Mississippi Region. Great Plains
F597	The Northwest
F598	Missouri River and Valley
F601-615	Minnesota
F616-630	Iowa
F631-645	North Dakota
F646-660	South Dakota
F661-675	Nebraska
F676-690	Kansas
F691-705	Oklahoma
F721-722	Rocky Mountains. Yellowstone National Park
F726-740	Montana
F741-755	Idaho
F756-770	Wyoming
F771-785	Colorado

United States local history - Continued

F786-790	New Southwest. Colorado River, Canyon, and Valley
F791-805	New Mexico
F806-820	Arizona
F821-835	Utah
F836-850	Nevada
F850.5-851.5	Pacific States
F851.7	Cascade Range
F852-854	Pacific Northwest. Columbia River and Valley. Northwest boundary since 1846
F856-870	California
F871-885	Oregon
F886-900	Washington
F901-951	Alaska
F951	Bering Sea and Aleutian Islands
F965	The territories of the United States (General)
F970	Insular possessions of the United States (General)
F975	Central American, West Indian, and other countries protected by and having close political affiliations with the United States (General)
F1001-1145.2	British America
F1001-1145.2	Canada
F1001-1035	General
F1035.8	Maritime provinces. Atlantic coast of Canada
F1036-1040	Nova Scotia. Acadia
F1041-1045	New Brunswick
F1046-1049.7	Prince Edward Island
F1050	St. Lawrence Gulf, River and Valley (General)
F1051-1055	Quebec
F1056-1059.7	Ontario
F1060-1060.97	Canadian Northwest. Northwest Territories
F1061-1065	Manitoba
F1067	Assiniboia
F1070-1074.7	Saskatchewan
F1075-1080	Alberta
F1086-1089.7	British Columbia
F1090	Rocky Mountains of Canada
F1090.5	Arctic regions
F1091-1095.5	Yukon
F1096-1100.5	Mackenzie
F1101-1105.7	Franklin
F1106-1110.5	Keewatin
F1121-1139	Newfoundland
F1135-1139	Labrador
F1140	The Labrador Peninsula
F1141-1145.2	Nunavut
F1170	French America
F1170	Saint Pierre and Miquelon
F1201-3799	Latin America. Spanish America
F1201-1392	Mexico
F1218.5-1221	Antiquities. Indians

F1401-1419	Latin America (General)
F1421-1440	Central America
F1435-1435.3	Mayas
F1441-1457	Belize
F1461-1477	Guatemala
F1481-1497	Salvador (El Salvador)
F1501-1517	Honduras
F1521-1537	Nicaragua
F1541-1557	Costa Rica
F1561-1577	Panama
F1569.C2	Canal Zone. Panama Canal
F1601-1629	West Indies
F1630-1640	Bermudas
F1650-1660	Bahamas
F1741-1991	Greater Antilles
F1751-1854.9	Cuba
F1861-1896	Jamaica
F1900-1941	Haiti (Island). Hispaniola
F1912-1930	Haiti (Republic)
F1931-1941	Dominican Republic
F1951-1983	Puerto Rico
F1991	Navassa
F2001-2151	Lesser Antilles
	Groups of islands, by geographical distribution
F2006	Leeward islands
F2011	Windward Islands
F2016	Islands along Venezuela coast
F2033-2129	Individual islands
	Groups of islands, by political allegiance
F2131-2133	British West Indies
F2136	Virgin Islands of the United States
F2141	Netherlands West Indies. Dutch West Indies
F2151	French West Indies
F2155-2191	Caribbean area. Caribbean Sea
F2201-3799	South America
F2201-2239	General
F2251-2299	Colombia
F2301-2349	Venezuela
F2351	Guiana
F2361-2391	Guyana. British Guiana
F2401-2431	Surinam
F2441-2471	French Guiana
F2501-2659	Brazil
F2661-2699	Paraguay
F2701-2799	Uruguay
F2801-3021	Argentina
F3031-3031.5	Falkland Islands
F3051-3285	Chile
F3301-3359	Bolivia
F3401-3619	Peru
F3701-3799	Ecuador

CLASS G - GEOGRAPHY. ANTHROPOLOGY. RECREATION

Subclass G

G1-922	Geography (General)
G80-99	History of geography
G100.5-108.5	Toponymy
	Including gazetteers, geographic names and terms
G140	Great cities of the world
G141	Historical geography
G142	Aerial geography
G149-180	Travel. Voyages and travels (General)
G154.9-180	Travel and state. Tourism
G200-336	History of discoveries, explorations, and travel
G369-503	Special voyages and travels
G521-539	Adventures, shipwrecks, buried treasure, etc.
G540-550	Seafaring life, ocean travel, etc.
G575-890	Arctic and Antarctic regions
G905-910	Tropics (General)
G912-922	Northern and Southern Hemispheres
G1000-3122	Atlases
G1000-1000.5	Atlases of the moon, planets, etc.
G1001-1046	World atlases
G1050-1052	Northern and Southern Hemispheres
G1053	Tropics. Torrid zone
G1054-1055	Polar regions
G1059-1061	Maritime atlases (General)
G1100-3102	By region or country
G1100-1779	America. Western Hemisphere
G1105-1692	North America
G1700-1779	South America
G1780-2799	Eastern Hemisphere. Eurasia, Africa, etc.
G1791-2082	Europe
G2110-2196	Former Soviet republics. Union of Soviet Socialist Republics (U.S.S.R.). Russia (Empire)
G2200-2444.84	Asia
G2445-2739	Africa
G2740-2799	Australasia
G2800-3064	Oceans (General)
G3100-3102	Antarctica
G3122	Atlases of imaginary, literary, and mythological regions, etc., A-Z
G3160-3171	Globes
G3180-9980	Maps
G3180-3182	Universe. Solar system
G3190-3192	Celestial maps
G3195-3199	Moon
G3200-3202	World
G3210-3222	Northern and Southern Hemispheres
G3240-3241	Tropics. Torrid zone
G3250-3251	Temperate Zone
G3260-3272	Polar regions

G3290-9880	By region or country
G3290-5668	America. Western Hemisphere
G3300-5184	North America
G5200-5668	South America
G5670-9084	Eastern Hemisphere. Eurasia, Africa, etc.
G5700-6967	Europe
G7000-7342	Former Soviet republics. Union of Soviet Socialist Republics (U.S.S.R.). Russia (Empire)
G7400-8198.54	Asia
G8200-8904	Africa
G8950-9084	Australasia
G9095-9794	Oceans (General)
G9800-9804	Antarctica
G9900-9980	Unlocalized maps

Subclass GA

GA1-1776	Mathematical geography. Cartography
GA51-87	Surveys (General)
GA101-1776	Cartography
GA110-115	Projection
GA125-155	Map drawing, modeling, printing, reading, etc.
GA192-197.3	Collections of maps, globes, etc. Map libraries
GA197.5-198	Cartographers
GA260-288	Globe making. Globes
GA300-325	World maps, general atlases, etc.
GA341-1776	Maps. By region or country

Subclass GB

GB3-5030	Physical geography
GB400-649	Geomorphology. Landforms. Terrain
GB447	Climatic geomorphology
GB448	Slopes
GB450-460	Coasts
GB461-468.995	Reefs
GB471-478.995	Islands
GB500-555	Mountains. Orography
GB561-649	Other natural landforms: Floodplains, caves, deserts, dunes, etc.
GB651-2998	Hydrology. Water
GB980-2998	Ground and surface waters
GB980-992	Watersheds. Runoff. Drainage
GB1001-1199.8	Groundwater. Hydrogeology
GB1201-1598	Rivers. Stream measurements
GB1601-2398	Lakes. Limnology. Ponds. Lagoons
GB2401-2598	Ice. Glaciers. Ice sheets. Sea ice
GB2601-2798	Snow. Snow surveys
GB2801-2998	Hydrometeorology
GB5000-5030	Natural disasters

Subclass GC

GC1-1581	Oceanography
GC65-78	Underwater exploration
GC83-87.6	Submarine topography
GC96-97.8	Estuarine oceanography
GC100-103	Seawater
GC109-149	Chemical oceanography
GC150-182	Physical oceanography
GC190-190.5	Ocean-atmosphere interaction
GC200-376	Dynamics of the ocean
GC377-399	Marine sediments
GC401-881	Oceanography. By region
GC1000-1023	Marine resources. Applied oceanography
GC1080-1581	Marine pollution. Seawater pollution

Subclass GE

GE1-350	Environmental sciences
GE70-90	Environmental education
GE170-190	Environmental policy
GE195-199	Environmentalism. Green movement
GE300-350	Environmental management

Subclass GF

GF1-900	Human ecology. Anthropogeography
GF51-71	Environmental influences on humans
GF75	Human influences on the environment
GF101-127	Settlements
GF125	Cities. Urban geography
GF127	Rural settlements. Rural geography
GF500-900	By region or country

Subclass GN

GN1-890	Anthropology
GN49-298	Physical anthropology. Somatology
GN51-59	Anthropometry
GN62.8-265	Human variation
GN269-279	Race (General)
GN281-289	Human evolution
GN296-296.5	Medical anthropology
GN301-674	Ethnology. Social and cultural anthropology
GN357-367	Culture and cultural processes
	Including social change, structuralism, diffusion, etc.
GN378-396	Collected ethnographies
GN397-397.5	Applied anthropology
GN406-517	Cultural traits, customs, and institutions
GN537-674	Ethnic groups and races
GN700-890	Prehistoric archaeology

Subclass GR

GR1-950	Folklore
GR72-79	Folk literature (General)
	Including folktales, legends
GR81	Folk beliefs, superstitions, etc. (General)
GR99.6-390	By region or country
GR420-950	By subject
GR420-426	Costume, jewelry
GR430-487	Folklore relating to private life
	Including dreams, love, children, nursery rhymes, etc.
GR500-615	Supernatural beings, demonology, fairies, ghosts, charms, etc.
GR620-640	Cosmic phenomena
GR650-690	Geographical topics
GR700-860	Animals, plants, and minerals
GR865-874	Transportation, travel, commerce, etc.
GR880	Medicine. Folk medicine
GR890-915	Occupations
GR931-935	Signs and symbols
GR940-941	Mythical places

Subclass GT

GT1-7070	Manners and customs (General)
GT165-476	Houses. Dwellings
GT485	Churches and church going
GT495-499	Human body and its parts. Personal beauty
GT500-2370	Costume. Dress. Fashion
GT2400-3390.5	Customs relative to private life
	Including children, marriage, eating and drinking, funeral customs, etc.
GT3400-5090	Customs relative to public and social life
	Including town life, court life, festivals, holidays, ceremonies of royalty, etc.
GT5220-5286	Customs relative to transportation and travel
GT5320-6737	Customs relative to special classes
GT5320-5690	By birth, rank, etc.
GT5750-6390	By occupation

Subclass GV

GV1-1860	Recreation. Leisure
GV181.35-181.6	Recreation leadership. Administration of recreation services
GV182-182.5	Recreational areas and facilities. Recreation centers
GV191.2-200.66	Outdoor life. Outdoor recreation
GV191.68-198.93	Camping
GV198.945-198.975	Dude ranches
GV199-199.62	Hiking. Pedestrian tours
GV199.8-200.35	Mountaineering
GV200.4-200.56	Orienteering. Wilderness survival
GV200.6-200.66	Caving. Spelunking

GV201-555	Physical education and training
GV346-351.5	School and college athletics. Intramural and interscholastic athletics
GV401-433	Physical education facilities. Sports facilities
	Including gymnasiums, athletic fields, playgrounds, etc.
GV435-436.7	Physical measurements. Physical tests, etc.
GV450-451.4	Nudism. Sunbathing
GV460-555	Gymnastics. Gymnastic exercises
	Including calisthenics, heavy exercises, acrobatics, etc.
GV557-1198.995	Sports
GV711	Coaching
GV712-725	Athletic contests. Sports events
GV733-734.5	Professionalism in sports. Professional sports (General)
GV735	Umpires. Sports officiating
GV743-749	Athletic and sporting goods, supplies, etc.
GV750-770.27	Air sports: Airplane flying, kiteflying, bungee jumping, etc.
GV770.3-840	Water sports: Canoeing, sailing, yachting, scuba diving, etc.
GV840.7-857	Winter sports: Ice hockey, skiing, bobsledding, snowmobiling, etc.
GV861-1017	Ball games: Baseball, football, golf, etc.
GV1020-1038.2	Automobile travel. Motoring. Automobile racing
GV1040-1060.4	Cycling. Bicycling. Motorcycling
GV1060.5-1098	Track and field athletics
GV1100-1150.9	Fighting sports: Bullfighting, boxing, fencing, etc.
GV1151-1190	Shooting. Archery
GV1195-1198.995	Wrestling
GV1199-1570	Games and amusements
GV1201.5	Hobbies (General)
GV1203-1218	Children's games and amusements
GV1218.5-1220.8	Toys
GV1221-1469.62	Indoor games and amusements
GV1232-1299	Card games: Poker, patience, whist, etc.
GV1301-1311	Gambling. Chance and banking games
GV1312-1469	Board games. Move games
	Including chess, go, checkers, etc.
GV1469.15-1469.62	Computer games. Video games. Fantasy games
GV1470-1511	Parties. Party games and stunts
GV1491-1507	Puzzles
GV1541-1561	Parlor magic and tricks
GV1564-1565	Darts
GV1580-1799.4	Dancing
GV1800-1860	Circuses, spectacles, etc.
	Including rodeos, waxworks, amusement parks, etc.

CLASS H - SOCIAL SCIENCES

Subclass H

H1-99	Social sciences (General)

Subclass HA

HA1-4737	Statistics
HA29-32	Theory and method of social science statistics
HA36-37	Statistical services. Statistical bureaus
HA38-39	Registration of vital events. Vital records
HA154-4737	Statistical data
HA154-155	Universal statistics
HA175-473	By region or country

Subclass HB

HB1-3840	Economic theory. Demography
HB71-74	Economics as a science. Relation to other subjects
HB75-130	History of economics. History of economic theory
	Including special economic schools
HB131-147	Methodology
HB201-206	Value. Utility
HB221-236	Price
HB238-251	Competition. Production. Wealth
HB501	Capital. Capitalism
HB522-715	Income. Factor shares
HB801-843	Consumption. Demand
HB846-846.8	Welfare theory
HB848-3697	Demography. Population. Vital events
HB3711-3840	Business cycles. Economic fluctuations

Subclass HC

HC10-1085	Economic history and conditions
HC79	Special topics
	Including air pollution, automation, consumer demand, famines, flow of funds, etc.
HC92	Economic geography of the oceans (General)
HC94-1085	By region or country

Subclass HD

HD28-9999	Industries. Land use. Labor
HD28-70	Management. Industrial management
HD72-88	Economic growth, development, planning
HD101-1395.5	Land use
HD1241-1339	Land tenure
HD1361-1395.5	Real estate business

Industries. Land use. Labor - Continued

HD1401-2210	Agriculture
HD1428-1431	International cooperation
HD1470-1476	Size of farms
HD1478	Sharecropping
HD1483-1486	Agricultural associations, societies, etc.
HD1491-1491.5	Cooperative agriculture
HD1492-1492.5	Collective farms
HD1493-1493.5	Government owned and operated farms. State farms. Sovkhozes
HD1501-1542	Agricultural classes
	Including farm tenancy, agricultural laborers
HD1549	Gleaning
HD1580	Reclamation of agricultural land. Melioration
HD1635-1702	Utilization and culture of special classes of lands
	Including pasture lands, water resources development
HD1711-1741	Irrigation
HD2321-4730.9	Industry
HD2329	Industrialization
HD2330	Rural industries
HD2331-2336	Home labor. Home-based businesses
HD2337-2339	Sweatshops
HD2340.8-2346.5	Small and medium-sized businesses, artisans, handicrafts, trades
HD2350.8-2356	Large industry. Factory system. Big business
HD2365-2385	Contracting. Letting of contracts
HD2421-2429	Trade associations
HD2709-2930.7	Corporations
	Including international business enterprises, diversification, industrial concentration, public utilities
HD2951-3575	Cooperation. Cooperative societies
HD3611-4730.9	Industrial policy. The state and industrial organization
	Including licensing of occupations and professions, subsidies, inspection, government ownership, municipal services
HD4801-8943	Labor. Work. Working class
HD4861-4895	Labor systems
HD4909-5100.9	Wages
HD5106-5267	Hours of labor
	Including overtime, shift work, sick leave, vacations
HD5306-5474	Labor disputes. Strikes and lockouts
HD5481-5630.7	Industrial arbitration. Mediation and conciliation
HD5650-5660	Employee participation in management. Employee ownership. Industrial democracy. Works councils
HD5701-6000.9	Labor market. Labor supply. Labor demand
	Including unemployment, manpower policy, occupational training, employment agencies
HD6050-6305	Classes of labor
	Including women, children, students, middle-aged and older persons, minorities
HD6350-6940.7	Trade unions. Labor unions. Workers' associations
HD6941-6948	Employers' associations

Labor. Work. Working class - Continued

HD6951-6957	Industrial sociology. Social conditions of labor
HD6958.5-6976	Industrial relations
HD6977-7080	Cost and standard of living
HD7088-7252	Social insurance. Social security. Pension
HD7255-7256	Vocational rehabilitation. Employment of people with disabilities
HD7260-7780.8	Industrial hygiene. Industrial welfare
HD7795-8027	Labor policy. Labor and the state
HD8031	Labor in politics. Political activity of the working class
HD8038	Professions (General). Professional employees
HD8039	By industry or trade
HD8045-8943	By region or country
HD9000-9999	Special industries and trades
HD9000-9495	Agricultural industries
HD9502-9502.5	Energy industries. Energy policy. Fuel trade
HD9506-9624	Mineral industries. Metal trade
HD9650-9663	Chemical industries
HD9665-9675	Pharmaceutical industry
HD9680-9714	Mechanical industries
	Including electric utilities, electronic industries, and machinery
HD9715-9717.5	Construction industry
HD9720-9975	Manufacturing industries
HD9999	Miscellaneous industries and trades

Subclass HE

HE1-9990	Transportation and communications
HE199-199.5	Freight (General)
HE199.9	Passenger traffic (General)
HE305-311	Urban transportation
HE323-328	Transportation geography. Trade routes
HE331-380	Traffic engineering. Roads and highways. Streets
HE374-377	Bridges
HE379-380	Tunnels. Vehicular tunnels
HE380.8-971	Water transportation
HE380.8-560	Waterways
HE561-971	Shipping
HE730-943	Merchant marine. Ocean shipping. Coastwise shipping
HE1001-5600	Railroads. Rapid transit systems
HE5601-5725	Automotive transportation
	Including trucking, bus lines, and taxicab service
HE5746-5749	Stage lines
HE5751-5870	Ferries
HE5880-5990	Express service
HE6000-7500	Postal service. Stamps. Philately
HE7511-7549	Pneumatic service

Subclass HG

HG1-9999	Finance
HG178	Liquidity
HG179	Personal finance
HG201-1496	Money
HG451-1496	By region or country
HG1501-3550	Banking
HG1621-1638	Interest rates. Interest tables
HG1641-1643	Bank loans. Bank credit. Commercial loans
HG1656	Bank reserves. Bank liquidity. Loan loss reserves
HG1660	Bank accounts. Bank deposits. Deposit banking
HG1662	Insurance of deposits. Deposit insurance
HG1685-1704	Drafts. Checks
HG1706-1708	Accounting. Bookkeeping
HG1710-1710.5	Electronic funds transfers
HG1811-2351	Special classes of banks and financial institutions
HG2397-3550	By region or country
HG3691-3769	Credit. Debt. Loans
	Including credit institutions, credit instruments, consumer credit, bankruptcy
HG3810-4000	Foreign exchange. International finance.
HG3879-3898	International monetary system
HG4001-4285	Finance management. Business finance. Corporation finance
HG4301-4480.9	Trust services. Trust companies
HG4501-6051	Investment, capital formation, speculation
HG4530	Investment companies. Investment trusts. Mutual funds
HG4538	Foreign investments
HG4551-4598	Stock exchanges
HG4621	Stockbrokers. Security dealers. Investment advisers
HG4701-4751	Government securities. Industrial securities. Venture capital
HG4900-5993	By region or country
HG6001-6051	Speculation
HG6105-6270.9	Lotteries
HG8011-9999	Insurance
HG8053.5-8054.45	Insurance for professions. Malpractice insurance. Professional liability insurance
HG8059	Business insurance
HG8075-8107	Insurance business. Insurance management
HG8111-8123	Government policy. State supervision
HG8205-8220	Government insurance
HG8501-8745	By region or country
HG8751-9295	Life insurance
HG9291-9295	Maternity insurance
HG9301-9343	Accident insurance
HG9371-9399	Health insurance
HG9651-9899	Fire insurance
HG9956-9969	Casualty insurance
HG9969.5-9999	Other insurance
	Including automobile, burglary, credit, disaster, title insurance

Subclass HJ

HJ9-9940	Public finance
HJ241-1620	By region or country
HJ2005-2216	Income and expenditure. Budget
HJ2240-5908	Revenue. Taxation. Internal revenue
HJ2321-2323	Tax incidence. Tax shifting. Tax equity
HJ2326-2327	Progressive taxation
HJ2336-2337	Tax exemption
HJ2338	Taxation of government property
HJ2351	Inflation and taxation
HJ2351.4	Tax revenue estimating
HJ2361-3192.7	By region or country
HJ3801-3844	Revenue from sources other than taxation
HJ3863-3925	Direct taxation
HJ4113-4601	Property tax
HJ4629-4830	Income tax
HJ4919-4936	Capitation. Poll tax
HJ5309-5510	Administrative fees. User charges. License fees
HJ6603-7390	Customs administration
HJ7461-7980	Expenditures. Government spending
HJ8001-8899	Public debts
HJ8052	Sinking funds. Amortization
HJ8101-8899	By region or country
HJ9103-9695	Local finance. Municipal finance
	Including the revenue, budget, expenditures of counties, boroughs, communes, municipalities, etc.
HJ9701-9940	Public accounting. Auditing

Subclass HM

HM401-1281	Sociology (General)
HM435-477	History of sociology. History of sociological theory
HM461-473	Schools of sociology. Schools of social thought
HM481-554	Theory. Method. Relations to other subjects
HM621-656	Culture
HM661-696	Social control
HM701	Social systems
HM706	Social structure
HM711-806	Groups and organizations
HM756-781	Community
HM786-806	Organizational sociology. Organization theory
HM811-821	Deviant behavior. Social deviance
HM826	Social institutions
HM831-901	Social change
HM1001-1281	Social psychology
HM1041-1101	Social perception. Social cognition
	Including perception of the self and others, prejudices, stereotype
HM1106-1171	Interpersonal relations. Social behavior
HM1176-1281	Social influence. Social pressure

Subclass HN

HN1-995	Social history and conditions. Social problems. Social reform
HN30-39	The church and social problems
HN41-46	Community centers. Social centers
HN50-995	By region or country

Subclass HQ

HQ1-2044	The Family. Marriage. Women
HQ12-449	Sexual life
HQ19-30.7	Sexual behavior and attitudes. Sexuality
HQ31-64	Sex instruction and sexual ethics
HQ101-440.7	Prostitution
HQ450-472	Erotica
HQ503-1064	The family. Marriage. Home
HQ750-755.5	Eugenics
HQ755.7-759.92	Parents. Parenthood
HQ760-767.7	Family size
HQ767.8-792.2	Children. Child development
	Including child rearing, child care, child life
HQ793-799.2	Youth. Adolescents. Teenagers
HQ799.5-799.9	Young men and women
HQ799.95-799.97	Adulthood
HQ800-800.4	Single people
HQ801-801.83	Man-woman relationships. Courtship. Dating
HQ802	Matrimonial bureaus. Marriage brokerage
HQ802.5	Matrimonial advertisements
HQ803	Temporary marriage. Trial marriage. Companionate marriage
HQ804	Breach of promise
HQ805	Desertion
HQ806	Adultery
HQ811-960.7	Divorce
HQ961-967	Free love
HQ981-996	Polygamy
HQ997	Polyandry
HQ998-999	Illegitimacy. Unmarried mothers
HQ1001-1006	The state and marriage
HQ1051-1057	The church and marriage
HQ1058-1058.5	Widows and widowers. Widowhood
HQ1060-1064	Aged. Gerontology (Social aspects). Retirement
HQ1073-1073.5	Thanatology. Death. Dying
HQ1075-1075.5	Sex role
HQ1088-1090.7	Men
HQ1101-2030.7	Women. Feminism
HQ1451-1870.7	By region or country
HQ1871-2030.7	Women's clubs
HQ2035-2039	Life skills. Coping skills. Everyday living skills
HQ2042-2044	Life style

Subclass HS

HS1-3371	Societies: secret, benevolent, etc.
HS101-330.7	Secret societies
HS351-929	Freemasons
HS951-1179	Odd Fellows
HS1201-1350	Knights of Pythias
HS1355	Other societies
HS1501-2460.7	Other societies. By classes
HS1501-1510	Benevolent and "friendly" societies and mutual assessment fraternities
HS1525-1560	Religious societies
HS1601-2265	Race societies
HS2275	Occupation societies
HS2301-2460.7	Political and "patriotic" societies
HS2501-3371	Clubs. Clubs and societies for special classes Including boys' societies, Boy scouts, girls' societies

Subclass HT

HT51-1595	Communities. Classes. Races
HT51-65	Human settlements. Communities
HT101-395	Urban groups. The city. Urban sociology
HT161-165	Garden cities. "The city beautiful"
HT165.5-169.9	City planning
HT170-178	Urban renewal. Urban redevelopment
HT201-221	City population Including children in cities, immigration
HT231	Effect of city life
HT251-265	Mental and moral life
HT281	Recreation. Amusements
HT321-325	The city as an economic factor. City promotion
HT330-334	Metropolitan areas
HT351-352	Suburban cities and towns
HT361-384	Urbanization. City and country
HT388	Regional economics. Space in economics
HT390-395	Regional planning
HT401-485	Rural groups. Rural sociology
HT601-1445	Classes
HT621-635	Origin of social classes
HT641-657	Classes arising from birth
HT675-690	Classes arising from occupation
HT713-725	Caste system
HT731	Freedmen
HT751-815	Serfdom
HT851-1445	Slavery
HT1048-1444	By region or country
HT1501-1595	Races Including race as a social group and race relations in general

HV1-9960	Social pathology. Social and public welfare. Criminology
HV40-69	Social service. Social work. Charity organization and practice
	Including social case work, private and public relief, institutional care, rural social work, work relief
HV85-525	By region or country
HV530	The church and charity
HV541	Women and charity
HV544	Charity fairs, bazaars, etc.
HV544.5	International social work
HV547	Self-help groups
HV551.2-639	Emergency management
HV553-639	Relief in case of disasters
HV560-583	Red Cross. Red Crescent
HV599-639	Special types of disasters
HV640-645	Refugee problems
HV650-670	Life saving
HV675-677	Accidents. Prevention of accidents
HV680-696	Free professional services
	Including medical charities
HV697-4959	Protection, assistance and relief
HV697-3024	Special classes
HV697-700.7	Families. Mothers. Widow's pensions
HV701-1420.5	Children
HV835-847	Foundlings
HV873-887	Destitute, neglected, and abandoned children. Street children
HV888-907	Children with disabilities
HV931-941	Fresh-air funds
HV959-1420.5	Orphanages. Orphans
HV1421-1441	Young adults. Youth. Teenagers
HV1442-1448	Women
HV1449	Gay men. Lesbians
HV1450-1494	Aged
HV1551-3024	People with disabilities
	Including blind, deaf, people with physical and mental disabilities
HV3025-3174	Special classes. By occupation
HV3025-3163	Mariners
HV3165-3173	Shop women, clerks, etc.
HV3174	Other. By occupation
HV3176-3199	Special classes. By race or ethnic group
HV4005-4013	Immigrants
HV4023-4470.7	Poor in cities. Slums
HV4480-4630	Mendicancy. Vagabondism. Tramps. Homelessness
HV4701-4890.9	Protection of animals. Animal rights. Animal welfare
HV4905-4959	Animal experimentation. Anti-vivisection
HV4961-4995	Degeneration
HV4997-5000	Substance abuse
HV5001-5720.5	Alcoholism. Intemperance. Temperance reform
HV5725-5770	Tobacco habit

HV5800-5840	Drug habits. Drug abuse
HV6001-7220.5	Criminology
HV6035-6197	Criminal anthropology
	Including criminal types, criminal psychology, prison psychology, causes of crime
HV6201-6249	Criminal classes
HV6250-6250.4	Victims of crimes. Victimology
HV6251-6773.55	Crimes and offenses
HV6774-7220.5	Crimes and criminal classes
HV7231-9960	Criminal justice administration
HV7428	Social work with delinquents and criminals
HV7431	Prevention of crime, methods, etc.
HV7435-7439	Gun control
HV7551-8280.7	Police. Detectives. Constabulary
HV7935-8025	Administration and organization
HV8031-8080	Police duty. Methods of protection
HV8079.5-8079.55	Traffic control. Traffic accident investigation
HV8081-8099	Private detectives. Detective bureaus
HV8130-8280.7	By region or country
HV8290-8291	Private security services
HV8301-9920.7	Penology. Prisons. Corrections
HV9051-9230.7	The juvenile offender. Juvenile delinquency. Reform schools, etc.
HV9261-9430.7	Reformation and reclamation of adult prisoners
HV9441-9920.7	By region or country
HV9950-9960	By region or country

Subclass HX

HX1-970.7	Socialism. Communism. Anarchism
HX519-550	Communism/socialism in relation to special topics
HX626-696	Communism: Utopian socialism, collective settlements
HX806-811	Utopias. The ideal state
HX821-970.9	Anarchism

CLASS J - POLITICAL SCIENCE

Subclass J

J1-981	General legislative and executive papers
J1-9	Gazettes: The Library of Congress now classes this material in K
	United States
J80-82	Presidents' messages and other executive papers
J100-981	Other regions and countries

Subclass JA

JA1-92	Political science (General)

Subclass JC

JC11-605	Political theory
JC11-605	State. Theories of the state
JC47	Oriental state
JC49	Islamic state
JC51-93	Ancient state
JC109-121	Medieval state
JC131-273	Modern state
JC311-314	Nationalism. Nation state
JC319-323	Political geography
JC327	Sovereignty
JC328.2	Consent of the governed
JC328.6	Violence. Political violence
JC329	Patriotism
JC345-347	Symbolism
JC348-497	Forms of the state
JC501-605	Purpose, functions, and relations of the state

Subclass JF

JF20-2112	Political institutions and public administration
JF20-1177	General. Comparative government
JF225-619	Organs and functions of government
JF251-289	Executive. Heads of state
JF331-341	Parliamentary government
JF491-619	Legislation. Legislative process. Law-making
JF800-1177	Political rights. Political participation
JF1338-2112	Public administration
JF1501-1521	Civil service
JF2011-2112	Political parties

Subclass JJ

JJ1000-1019.Z8	Political institutions and public administration: North America

Subclass JK

JK1-9993	Political institutions and public administration
JK1-9593	United States
JK404-1685	Government. Public administration
JK501-868	Executive branch
JK631-868	Civil Service. Departments and agencies
JK1012-1432	Congress. Legislative branch
JK1154-1276	Senate
JK1308-1443	House of Representatives
JK1606-1685	Government property, etc.
JK1717-2217	Political rights. Practical politics
JK1758-1761	Citizenship
JK1846-1929	Suffrage
JK1965-2217	Electoral system
JK2255-2391	Political parties
JK2403-9593	State government
JK9663-9993	Confederate States of America

Subclass JL

JL1-3899	Political institutions and public administration
JL1-500	Canada
JL599.5-839	West Indies. Caribbean Area
JL1200-1299	Mexico
JL1400-1679	Central America
JL1850-3899	South America

Subclass JN

JN1-9689	Political institutions and public administration: Europe
JN1-97	Europe (General)
JN101-1179	Great Britain
JN1187-1371	Scotland
JN1405-1571.5	Ireland
JN1601-2191	Austria-Hungary. Austria. Hungary
JN2210-2229	Czech Republic. Czechoslovakia
JN2240	Slovakia
JN2301-3007	France
JN3201-4944	Germany
JN5001-5191	Greece
JN5201-5690	Italy
JN5701-5999	Netherlands
JN6101-6371	Belgium
JN6500-6598	Soviet Union. Russia. Former Soviet Republics
JN6615	Estonia
JN6630-6639	Ukraine
JN6640-6649	Belarus
JN6680-6689	Moldova
JN6690-6699	Russia (Federation)
JN6730-6739	Latvia

JN6745	Lithuania
JN6750-6769	Poland
JN7011-7066	Scandinavia. Northern Europe
JN7101-7367	Denmark
JN7370-7379	Greenland
JN7380-7389	Iceland
JN7390-7399	Finland
JN7401-7695	Norway
JN7721-7995	Sweden
JN8101-8399	Spain
JN8423-8661	Portugal
JN8701-9599	Switzerland
JN9600-9689	Balkan States

Subclass JQ

JQ21-6651	Political institutions and public administration
JQ21-1849	Asia
JQ200-620	India
JQ1070-1199	Central Asia
	Including former republics of the Soviet Union
JQ1499-1749	East Asia
JQ1758-1852	Middle East
JQ1850	Arab countries
JQ1852	Islamic countries
JQ1870-3981	Africa
JQ3981.5-3986.7	Atlantic Ocean islands
JQ3995-6651	Australia. New Zealand. Pacific Ocean islands

Subclass JS

JS39-8500	Local government. Municipal government
JS55-67	History
JS141-271	Municipal government and local government other than municipal
JS300-1583	United States
JS1701-1800	Canada
JS1840-2058	West Indies. Caribbean Area
JS2101-2143	Mexico
JS2145-2219	Central America
JS2300-2778	South America
JS3000-6949.8	Europe
JS6950-7509	Asia
JS7510	Arab countries
JS7520	Islamic countries
JS7525-7819	Africa
JS7820-7827	Atlantic Ocean islands
JS7900-7906	Indian Ocean islands
JS8001-8490	Australia. New Zealand. Pacific Ocean islands

Subclass JV

JV1-9480	Colonies and colonization. Emigration and immigration. International migration
JV1-5399	Colonies and colonization
JV61-151	History
JV500-5399	Colonizing nations
JV6001-9480	Emigration and immigration. International migration
JV6403-7127	United States
JV7200-7539	Canada, Latin America, etc.
JV7590-8339.7	Europe
JV8490-8758	Asia
JV8760	Arab countries
JV8762	Islamic countries
JV8790-9024.5	Africa
JV9029-9036	Atlantic Ocean islands
JV9040-9047	Indian Ocean islands
JV9100-9269	Australia. New Zealand
JV9290-9470	Pacific Ocean islands

Subclass JX (obsolete)

JX(1-6650)	International law, see KZ

Subclass JZ

JZ5-6530	International relations
JZ63-1153	Sources
JZ221-1153	By region or country
JZ1249-1254	Relation to other disciplines and topics
JZ1305-2060	Scope of international relations
JZ1329.5-1395	By period
JZ1400-1454	Diplomatic and consular service
JZ1464-2060	By country, territory, or region
JZ3675-3875	State territory and its different parts
JZ3685	Boundaries
JZ3686-3875	International waters
JZ4835-5490	International organizations and associations
JZ4841-4848	Political non-governmental organizations. NGOs
JZ4850-5490	Intergovernmental organizations. IGOs
JZ4853-4934	The League of Nations
JZ4935-5160	The United Nations
JZ5511.2-6060	Promotion of peace. Peaceful change
JZ5587-6009	International security. Disarmament
JZ6010-6060	Pacific settlement of international disputes
JZ6360-6377	Non-military coercion
JZ6385-6405	The armed conflict. War and order
JZ6422-6422.5	Neutrality
JZ6530	Humanitarian aspects of war

Subclass K

K1-7720	Law in general. Comparative and uniform law. Jurisprudence
K201-487	Jurisprudence. Philosophy and theory of law
K524-5582	Comparative law. International uniform law
K524-525	Treaties and other international agreements
K540-546	Trials
K578-579	Concepts applying to several branches of law
K583-590.5	Legal systems compared
K592-597	Regional divisions. Interregional comparative law
K600-615	Private law
K623-968	Civil law
K970	Compensation to victims of crime. Reparation
K1000-1395	Commercial law
K1401-1578	Intellectual property
K1700-1973	Social legislation
K2100-2385	Courts. Procedure
K2390	Negotiated settlement. Compromise
K2400-2405	Arbitration and award
K3150	Public law
K3154-3370	Constitutional law
K3375	Colonial law
K3400-3431	Administrative law
K3440-3460	Civil service. Government officials and employees
K3476-3560	Public property. Public restraint on private property
K3566-3578	Public health
K3581-3597	Environmental law
K3601-3611	Medical legislation
K3615-3622	Veterinary laws. Veterinary medicine and hygiene. Prevention of cruelty to animals
K3625-3649	Food. Drugs. Cosmetics
K3651-3654	Alcohol. Alcoholic beverages
K3661-3674	Public safety
K3700-3705	Control of social activities
K3740-3762	Education
K3770-3795	Science and arts. Research
K3820-3836	Economic constitution, policy, planning, and development
K3840-4375	Regulation of industry, trade, and commerce. Occupational law
K4430-4675	Public finance
K4700-4705	Government measures in time of war, national emergency, or economic crisis
K4720-4780	National defense. Military law
K5000-5582	Criminal law and procedure
K7000-7720	Private international law. Conflict of laws
K7120-7197	Persons
K7200-7218	Property
K7222	Trust and trustees
K7230-7245	Succession upon death

	Law in general. Comparative and uniform law. Jurisprudence
	Private international law. Conflict of laws - Continued
K7260-7338	Obligations
K7340-7512	Commercial law
K7550-7582	Intellectual property
K7585-7595	Social legislation
K7611-7688	Civil procedure. International civil procedure
K7690	Arbitration and award
K7720	Recognition of foreign administrative acts

Subclass KB

Religious law in general. Comparative religious law. Jurisprudence (in development)

Subclass KBM

Jewish law

Subclass KBP

(1)-4860	Islamic law. Shar ī'ah. Fiqh
42-43	Legal education. Study and teaching
(49-49.5)	Historiography. Biography of scholars and historians
50-(75.4)	History, development and application of Islamic law
(100-136.8)	Sources. Qur'an. Hadith
144	General works
173.25-(173.6)	Islamic law and other disciplines and subjects
174-184.9	Observances and practice of Islam
250-420	Schools of thought. Islamic legal schools. Madhāhib
425-485	Usūl al-fiqh. Jurisprudence and theory of law
490-4860	Furū' al-fiqh. Substantive law. Branches of law
490-490.9	General works. Treatises
491-497	Particular genre. Fatwas. Hiyal. Shurūt
500-509.8	General concepts
524-638	Aḥwāl shakhṣīyah
639-1154	Mu'āmalāt
1155-1194	Intellectual and industrial property
1270-1467	Labor laws and legislation
1572-1942	Courts and procedure
2000-2035	Public law. The state and Islam
2101-2612	Constitution of the theocratic state. Constitutional law
2730-2968	Government and administration. Siyāsah. Administrative process
3000-3037	Police and public safety
3040.5-3073	Public property. Government property. Public land law
3075-3097	Public health
3098-3121.5	Medical legislation
3127-3135	Environmental law
3137-3183.3	Cultural affairs
3190-3430	Economic law
3440-3512	Transportation and communication
3515-3522	Professions. Intelligentsia
3526-3705	Public finance
3709-3727	Government measures in time of war, national emergency or economic crisis

KBU3075-3165	Sacraments. Administration of sacraments
KBU3180-3182	Sacramentals
KBU3184-3256	Other acts of divine worship
KBU3282-3310	Medical ethics and legislation
KBU3320-3460	Church property
KBU3500-3774	Sanctions in the Church. Criminal law
KBU3780-3985	Courts and procedure
KBU4000-4097	Church and state relationships
KBU4112-4820	Local Church government. By region or country

Subclass KD

KD	Law of the United Kingdom and Ireland
KD51-9500	England and Wales
KD8850-9312	Local laws of England
KD9320-9355	Local laws of Wales
KD9400-9500	Wales
KDC51-990	Scotland
KDE 21-580	Northern Ireland
KDG26-540	Isle of Man. Channel Islands
KDK21-1950	Ireland (Eire)

Subclass KDZ

KDZ1-4999	America. North America
KDZ1101-1199	Organization of American States (OAS)
KDZ2001-2499.2	Bermuda
KDZ3001-3499	Greenland
KDZ4001-4499	St. Pierre and Miquelon

Subclass KE

KE	Law of Canada
KE1-9450	Federal law. Common and collective provincial law
	Individual provinces and territories
KEA1-599	Alberta
KEB1-599	British Columbia
KEM1-599	Manitoba
KEN1-599	New Brunswick
KEN1201-1799	Newfoundland
KEN5401-5999	Northwest Territories
KEN7401-7999	Nova Scotia
KEO1-1199	Ontario
KEP1-599	Prince Edward Island
KEQ1-1199	Quebec
KES1-599	Saskatchewan
KEY1-599	Yukon Territory
KEZ1-9999	Individual cities, A-Z

Subclass KF

KF	Law of the United States
KF1-9827	Federal law. Common and collective state law
	Individual states
KFA1-599	Alabama
KFA1201-1799	Alaska
KFA2401-2999	Arizona
KFA3601-4199	Arkansas
KFC1-1199	California
KFC1801-2399	Colorado
KFC3601-4199	Connecticut
KFD1-599	Delaware
KFD1201-1799	District of Columbia
KFF1-599	Florida
KFG1-599	Georgia
KFH1-599	Hawaii
KFI1-599	Idaho
KFI1201-1799	Illinois
KFI3001-3599	Indiana
KFI4201-4799	Iowa
KFK1-599	Kansas
KFK1201-1799	Kentucky
KFL1-599	Louisiana
KFM1-599	Maine
KFM1201-1799	Maryland
KFM2401-2999	Massachusetts
KFM4201-4799	Michigan
KFM5401-5999	Minnesota
KFM6601-7199	Mississippi
KFM7801-8399	Missouri
KFM9001-9599	Montana
KFN1-599	Nebraska
KFN601-1199	Nevada
KFN1201-1799	New Hampshire
KFN1801-2399	New Jersey
KFN3601-4199	New Mexico
KFN5001-6199	New York
KFN7401-7999	North Carolina
KFN8601-9199	North Dakota
KFO1-599	Ohio
KFO1201-1799	Oklahoma
KFO2401-2999	Oregon
KFP1-599	Pennsylvania
KFR1-599	Rhode Island
KFS1801-2399	South Carolina
KFS3001-3599	South Dakota
KFT1-599	Tennessee
KFT1201-1799	Texas
KFU1-599	Utah
KFV1-599	Vermont
KFV2401-2999	Virginia

Individual states - Continued

KFW1-599	Washington
KFW1201-1799	West Virginia
KFW2401-2999	Wisconsin
KFW4201-4799	Wyoming
KFX1-9999	Individual cities, A-Z
KFZ1801-2399	Northwest Territory
KFZ8601-9199	Confederate States of America

Subclass KG

KG1-999	Latin America (General)
KG3001-3999	Mexico and Central America (General)
KGA1-9000	Belize
KGB1-9000	Costa Rica
KGC1-9800	El Salvador
KGD1-9990	Guatemala
KGE1-9990	Honduras
KGF1-9900	Mexico
KGG1-9800	Nicaragua
KGH1-8000	Panama
KGH9001-9499	Panama Canal Zone
	West Indies. Caribbean area
KGJ1-999	General
KGJ7001-7499	Anguilla
KGK1-499	Antigua and Barbuda
KGK1001-1499	Aruba
KGL1-499	Bahamas
KGL1001-1499	Barbados
KGL2001-2499	Bonaire
KGL3001-3499	British Leeward Islands
KGL4001-4499	British Virgin Islands
KGL5001-5999	British West Indies
KGL6001-6499	British Windward Islands
KGM1-499	Cayman Islands
KGN1-9800	Cuba
KGP1-499	Curaçao
KGP2001-2499	Dominica
KGQ1-9800	Dominican Republic
KGR1-499	Dutch Leeward Islands (General)
KGR1001-1499	Dutch West Indies (Netherlands Antilles)
KGR2001-2499	Dutch Windward Islands (General)
KGR3001-3499	French West Indies (General)
KGR4001-4499	Grenada
KGR5001-5499	Guadeloupe
KGS1-9000	Haiti
KGT1-499	Jamaica
KGT1001-1499	Martinique
KGT2001-2499	Montserrat
KGU1-499	Navassa Islands
KGV1-8200	Puerto Rico

KGW1-499	Saba
KGW2001-2499	Saint Christopher (Saint Kitts), Nevis, and Anguilla
KGW3001-3499	Saint Lucia
KGW5001-5499	Saint Vincent and the Grenadines
KGW7001-7499	Sint Eustatius
KGW8001-8499	Sint Maarten
KGX1-499	Trinidad and Tobago
KGY1-499	Turks and Caicos Islands
KGZ1-499	Virgin Islands of the United States

Subclass KH

KH1-999	South America (General)
KHA1-9800	Argentina
KHC1-8200	Bolivia
KHD1-9900	Brazil
KHF1-9800	Chile
KHH1-9900	Colombia
KHK1-9990	Ecuador
KHL1-9000	Falkland Islands
KHM1-9000	French Guiana
KHN1-9000	Guyana
KHP1-9700	Paraguay
KHQ1-9800	Peru
KHS1-9000	Surinam
KHU1-9800	Uruguay
KHW1-9900	Venezuela

Subclasses KJ-KKZ

KJ	Europe
KJ2-1040	History of Law
KJ160-1040	Germanic law
KJA2-3660	Roman law
KJC2-9799	Regional comparative and uniform law
KJE5-7975	Regional organization and integration. Comparative law
KJG1-4999	Albania
KJH1-499	Andorra
KJJ1-4999	Austria
KJK1-4999	Belgium
KJM1-4999	Bulgaria
KJN1-499	Cyprus
KJP1-4999	Czechoslovakia
KJR1-4999	Denmark
KJS1-4985	Estonia
KJT1-4999	Finland
	France
KJV2-9158	National laws
KJW51-4360	Individual regions, provinces, departments, etc.
KJW5201-9600	Individual cities

Law of Europe - Continued
Germany

KK2-9799.3	Germany and West Germany
KKA7-9796	East Germany
KKB-KKC	Individual states, provinces, and cities
KKE1-4999	Greece
KKF1-4999	Hungary
KKG1-499	Iceland
KKH1-4999	Italy
KKI1-4890	Latvia
KKJ1-499	Liechtenstein
KKJ501-9890	Lithuania
KKK1-499	Luxembourg
KKK1001-1499	Malta
KKL1-499	Monaco
KKM1-4999	Netherlands
KKN1-4999	Norway
KKP1-4999	Poland
KKQ1-4999	Portugal
KKR1-4999	Romania
KKS1-499	San Marino
KKT1-4999	Spain
KKW1-4999	Switzerland
KKX1-4999	Turkey
KKY1-4999	Ukraine (1991-)
KKZ1-4999	Yugoslavia

Subclass KL

	Asia and Eurasia, Africa, Pacific Area, and Antarctica
KL2-5915	History of law. The ancient orient
KL2-135	General
KL147-177	Ancient legal systems compared
KL190-420	Sources
KL700-2215	Mesopotamia. Assyro-Babylonian law
KL1000-1299	Sumer
KL1600-1899	Assyria
KL2200-2499	Babylonia
KL2800-3099	Egypt
KL3500-3799	Elam
KL4110-4399	Greek law
KL4700-4999	Hittite law
KL5300-5599	Persia
KL5900-6199	Phoenicia
	Eurasia
	Turkey, see KKX
KLA1-9999	Russia. Soviet Union
KLB1-6499	Russia (Federation, 1992-)
KLD1-490	Armenia (Republic)
KLE1-490	Azerbaijan
KLF1-490	Belarus (Republic)
	Estonia, see KJS

	Eurasia - Continued
KLH1-490	Georgia (Republic)
	Latvia, see KKI
	Lithuania, see KKJ
KLM1-490	Moldova
KLN1-489	Russian S.F.S.R. (to 1991)
KLP1-4989	Ukraine (1919-1991)
KLP9001-9499	Zakavkazskaia Sotsialisticheskaia Federativnaia Sovetskaia Respublika (to 1936)
KLQ1-499	Bukharskaia Narodnaia Sovetskaia Respublika (to 1924)
KLR1-490	Kazakhstan
KLR1001-1499	Khorezmskaia Sovetskaia Sotsialisticheskaia Respublika (to 1924)
KLS1-490	Kyrgyzstan
KLT1-490	Tadjikistan
KLV1-490	Turkmenistan
KLW1-490	Uzbekistan

Subclass KM

Asia and Eurasia, Africa, Pacific Area, and Antarctica

	Asia
KM1-999	General
	Middle East. Southwest Asia
KMC1-799	Regional comparative and uniform law
KMF1-293.5	Armenia (to 1921)
KMF1001-1490	Bahrain
KMG1-489	Gaza
KMH1-4990	Iran
KMJ1-4990	Iraq
KMK1-4990	Israel
KML1-490	Jerusalem
KMM1-490	Jordan
KMM501-994	West Bank (Territory under Israeli occupation, 1967-)
KMN1-499	Kuwait
KMP1-490	Lebanon
KMQ1-490	Oman
KMQ1001-1499	Palestine (to 1948)
KMS1-490	Qatar
KMT1-4990	Saudi Arabia
	Southern Yemen, see KMY
KMU1-490	Syria
KMV1-9870	United Arab Emirates
KMX1001-1526	Yemen
KMY1-489	Yemen (People's Democratic Republic) (to 1990)

Subclass KN

Asia and Eurasia, Africa, Pacific Area, and Antarctica
Asia
South Asia. Southeast Asia. East Asia

KNC1-999	Regional comparative and uniform law
KNE150-499	Regional organization and integration
KNF1-4990	Afghanistan
KNG1-4990	Bangladesh
KNH1-490	Bhutan
KNK1-490	Brunei
KNL1-4990	Burma
KNM1-4990	Cambodia
KNN1-9000	China
KNP1-599	China (Republic, 1949-). Taiwan
KNQ1-9665	China (People's Republic, 1949-)
KNR1-489	Hong Kong
KNS1-4999	India
KNT-KNU	States, cities, etc.
KNV1-489	French Indochina
KNW1-4990	Indonesia
KNX1-4999	Japan
KNY10-220	Cities, etc.

Subclass KP

Asia and Eurasia, Africa, Pacific Area, and Antarctica
Asia
South Asia. Southeast Asia. East Asia

KPA1-4990	Korea. South Korea
KPC1-4990	Democratic People's Republic of Korea. North Korea
KPE1-4990	Laos
KPF1-489	Macao
KPG1-6999	Malaysia
KPG7001-9999	States of East and West Malaysia (1957-)
KPH1-4990	States of East and West Malaysia (1957-)
KPH5001-5490	Maldives
KPJ1-490	Mongolia
KPK1-490	Nepal
KPL1-4990	Pakistan
KPM1-4990	Philippines
KPP1-499	Singapore
KPS1-4990	Sri Lanka
KPT1-4990	Thailand
KPV1-8094	Vietnam
KPW1-489	Vietnam. South Vietnam

Subclass KQ

	Asia and Eurasia, Africa, Pacific Area, and Antarctica
	Africa
KQ2-197	History of law
KQ2010-9000	Law of indigenous peoples
KQC1-999	Regional comparative and uniform law
KQE10-1249	Regional organization and integration
KQG1-4990	Algeria
KQH1-4990	Angola
KQJ1-490	Benin
KQK1-490	Botswana
KQM1-499	British Central Africa Protectorate
KQP1-499	British Indian Ocean Territory
KQP1001-1499	British Somaliland
KQT1-490	Burkina Faso
KQV1-490	Burundi
KQW1-8020	Cameroon
KQX1-490	Cape Verde

Subclass KR

	Asia and Eurasia, Africa, Pacific Area, and Antarctica
	Africa
KRB1-490	Central African Republic
KRC1-490	Chad
KRE1-490	Comoros
KRG1-490	Congo
KRK1-490	Djibouti
KRL1-499	East AFrica Protectorate
KRM1-4990	Egypt
KRP1-4990	Ethiopia
KRR1-499	French Equatorial Africa
KRS1-499	French West Africa
KRU1-490	Gabon
KRV1-489	Gambia
KRW1-499	German East Africa
KRX1-4990	Ghana
KRY1-499	Gibraltar

Subclass KS

	Asia and Eurasia, Africa, Pacific Area, and Antarctica
	Africa
KSA1-490	Guinea
KSC1-490	Guinea-Bissau
KSE1-490	Equatorial Guinea
KSE601-699	Ifni
KSG1-499	Italian East Africa
KSG1001-1499	Italian Somaliland
KSH1-4990	Ivory Coast

KSK1-4990	Kenya
KSL1-490	Lesotho
KSN1-490	Liberia
KSP1-4990	Libya
KSR1-490	Madagascar
KSS1-490	Malawi
KST1-490	Mali
KSU1-490	Mauritania
KSV1-490	Mauritius
KSV5001-5490	Mayotte
KSW1-4990	Morocco
KSX1-4990	Mozambique
KSY1-4990	Namibia
KSZ1-490	Niger

Subclass KT

Asia and Eurasia, Africa, Pacific Area, and Antarctica
Africa

KTA1-9150	Nigeria
KTC1-499	Réunion
KTD1-490	Rwanda
KTE1-490	Saint Helena
KTF1-490	São Tomé and Principe
KTG1-4990	Senegal
KTH1-490	Seychelles
KTJ1-490	Sierra Leone
KTK1-490	Somalia
KTL1-9560	South Africa, Republic of
KTN1-499	Spanish West Africa (to 1958)
KTN601-699	Spanish Sahara (to 1975)
KTQ1-4990	Sudan
KTR1-490	Swaziland
KTT1-9910	Tanzania
KTU1-490	Togo
KTV1-4990	Tunisia
KTW1-490	Uganda
KTX1-4990	Zaire
KTY1-490	Zambia
KTY1501-1599	Zanzibar (to 1964)
KTZ1-490	Zimbabwe

Subclass KU

	Asia and Eurasia, Africa, Pacific Area, and Antarctica
	Pacific Area
KU1-4999	Australia
KUA-KUH	States and territories
	External territories
KUN501-599	Norfolk Island
KUN3001-3050	Cities, communities, etc.
KUQ1-4990	New Zealand

Subclass KV

	Asia and Eurasia, Africa, Pacific Area, and Antarctica
	Pacific Area
	Pacific area jurisdictions
KVC1-999	Regional comparative and uniform law
KVE200-349	Regional organization and integration
KVH1-490	American Samoa
KVH1001-1499	British New Guinea (Territory of Papua)
KVL1-489	Cook Islands
KVM1-489	Easter Island
KVN1-490	Fiji
KVP1-100	French Polynesia
KVP1001-1099	German New Guinea (to 1914)
KVQ1-490	Guam
KVR1-490	Kiribati
KVS1-490	Marshall Islands
KVS501-990	Micronesia (Federated States)
KVS2501-2999	Midway Islands
KVU1-499	Nauru
KVU1001-1099	Netherlands New Guinea (to 1963)
KVW1-490	New Caledonia

Subclass KW

	Asia and Eurasia, Africa, Pacific Area, and Antarctica
	Pacific Area
	Pacific area jurisdictions
KWA1-489	Niue
KWC1-490	Northern Mariana Islands
KWE1-499	Pacific Islands (Trust Territory)
KWG1-490	Palau
KWH1-490	Papua New Guinea
KWL1-499	Pitcairn Island
KWL2001-2490	Solomon Islands
KWP1-490	Tonga
KWQ1-490	Tuvalu
KWR1-490	Vanuatu

Subclass KZ

CLASS L - EDUCATION

Subclass L

L7-991	Education (General)
L111-791	Official documents, reports, etc.
L797-898	Educational exhibitions and museums
L900-991	Directories of educational institutions

Subclass LA

LA5-2396	History of education
LA5-25	General
LA31-135	By period
LA173-186	Higher education
LA201-398	United States
LA410-2284	Other regions or countries
LA2301-2396	Biography

Subclass LB

LB5-3640	Theory and practice of education
LB5-45	General
LB51-885	Systems of individual educators and writers
LB1025-1050.75	Teaching (Principles and practice)
LB1049.9-1050.75	Reading (General)
LB1050.9-1091	Educational psychology
LB1101-1139	Child study
LB1139.2-1139.5	Early childhood education
LB1140-1140.5	Preschool education. Nursery schools
LB1141-1489	Kindergarten
LB1501-1547	Primary education
LB1555-1602	Elementary or public school education
LB1603-1696.6	Secondary education. High schools
LB1705-2286	Education and training of teachers and administrators
LB1805-2151	State teachers colleges
LB2165-2278	Teacher training in universities and colleges
LB2300-2430	Higher education
LB2326.4-2330	Institutions of higher education
LB2331.7-2335.8	Teaching personnel
LB2335.86-2335.885	Trade unions
LB2335.95-2337	Endowments, trusts, etc.
LB2337.2-2340.8	Student financial aid
LB2341-2341.95	Supervision and administration. Business management
LB2351-2359	Admissions and entrance requirements
LB2361-2365	Curriculum
LB2366-2367.75	College examinations
LB2371-2372	Graduate education
LB2381-2391	Academic degrees
LB2799-2799.3	Educational consultants and consulting

	Theory and practice of education - Continued
LB2801-3095	School administration and organization
LB2831.6-2831.99	Administrative personnel
LB2832-2844.1	Teaching personnel
LB2844.52-2844.63	Trade unions
LB3011-3095	School management and discipline
LB3045-3048	Textbooks
LB3050-3060.87	Educational tests, measurements, evaluations and examinations
LB3201-3325	School architecture and equipment. School physical facilities. Campus planning
LB3401-3495	School hygiene. School health services
LB3497-3499	Hygiene in universities and colleges
LB3525-3575	Special days
LB3602-3640	School life. Student manners and customs

Subclass LC

LC8-6691	Special aspects of education
LC8-59	Forms of education
LC8	General works
LC15	Conversation and culture
LC25-33	Self-education. Self-culture
LC37-44.3	Home education
LC45-45.8	Nonformal education
LC47-58.7	Private school education
LC59	Public school education
LC65-245	Social aspects of education
LC65-67.68	Economic aspects of education
LC68-70	Demographic aspects of education
LC71-120.4	Education and the state
LC72-72.5	Academic freedom
LC107-120.4	Public school question. Secularization. Religious instruction in the public schools
LC129-139	Compulsory education
LC142-148.5	Attendance. Dropouts
LC149-161	Literacy. Illiteracy
LC165-182	Higher education and the state
LC184-188	Taxation of schools and colleges
LC189-214.53	Educational sociology
LC215-238.4	Community and the school
LC241-245	Foundations, endowments, funds
LC251-951	Moral and religious education
LC251-318	Moral education. Character building
LC321-951	Religion and education. Education under church control
LC361-629	Christian education. Church education
LC701-775	Jewish education
LC901-915	Islamic education
LC921-929.7	Buddhist education

LC980-1099.5	Types of education
LC1001-1024	Humanistic education. Liberal education
LC1022-1022.25	Computer-assisted education
LC1025-1027	Collective education
LC1030	Communist education
LC1031-1034.5	Competency based education
LC1035-1035.8	Basic education. Basic skills education
LC1036-1036.8	Community education
LC1037-1037.8	Career education
LC1041-1048	Vocational education (General)
LC1049-1049.8	Cooperative education
LC1051-1072	Professional education
LC1081-1087.4	Industrial education (General)
LC1090-1091	Political education
LC1099-1099.5	Multicultural education (General)
LC1200-1203	Inclusive education
LC1390-5160.3	Education of special classes of persons
LC1390	Boys
LC1401-2572	Women
LC2574-2576	Gays. Lesbians. Bisexuals
LC2580-2582	Student-athletes
LC2601-2611	Education in developing countries
LC2630-2638	Asian Americans. Asians in the United States
LC2667-2698	Latin Americans. Hispanic Americans
LC2699-2913	Blacks. Afro-Americans
LC3001-3501	Asians
LC3503-3520	Gypsies
LC3530-3540	Lapps
LC3551-3593	Jews
LC3701-3740	Immigrants or ethnic and linguistic minorities. Bilingual schools and bilingual education
LC3745-3747	Children of immigrants (First generation)
LC3950-4806.5	Exceptional children and youth. Special education
LC4812-5160.3	Other special classes
LC5161-5163	Fundamental education
LC5201-6660.4	Education extension. Adult education. Continuing education
LC5451-5493	Aged education
LC5501-5560	Evening schools
LC5701-5771	Vacation schools. Summer schools
LC5800-5808	Distance education
LC5900-6101	Correspondence schools
LC6201-6401	University extension
LC6501-6560.4	Lyceums and lecture courses. Forums
LC6571-6581	Radio and television extension courses. Instruction by radio and television
LC6601-6660.4	Reading circles and correspondence clubs
LC6681	Education and travel
LC6691	Traveling educational exhibits

Subclass LD

LD13-7501	Individual institutions
LD13-7501	United States
LD13-7251	Universities. Colleges
LD6501	Community colleges. Junior colleges
LD7020-7251	Women's colleges
LD7501	Secondary and elementary schools

Subclass LE

LE3-78	Individual institutions
LE3-78	America (except United States)
LE3-5	Canada
LE7-9	Mexico
LE11-13	Central America
LE15-17	West Indies
LE21-78	South America
LE21-23	Argentina
LE27-29	Bolivia
LE31-33	Brazil
LE36-38	Chile
LE41-43	Colombia
LE46-48	Ecuador
LE51-59	Guianas
LE61-63	Paraguay
LE66-68	Peru
LE71-73	Uruguay
LE76-78	Venezuela

Subclass LF

LF14-5627	Individual institutions
LF14-1257	Great Britain
LF14-797	England
LF800-957	Ireland
LF960-1137	Scotland
LF1140-1257	Wales
LF1341-1537	Austria
LF1541-1549	Czech Republic
LF1550-1550.8	Slovakia
LF1561-1697	Hungary
LF1705-1709	Finland
LF1711-2397	France
LF2402-3197	Germany
LF3211-3247	Greece
LF3248-3897	Italy
LF3899	Malta
LF3911-4067	Belgium
LF4069	Luxembourg

LF4071-4197	Netherlands
LF4203-4209	Poland
LF4251-4437	Russia (Federation)
LF4440-4441	Estonia
LF4443-4444	Latvia
LF4445-4446	Lithuania
LF4447.2-4447.5	Belarus
LF4448-4448.5	Moldova
LF4449.2-4449.5	Ukraine
LF4451-4487	Denmark
LF4488-4488.2	Faroe Islands
LF4489-4491	Iceland
LF4493-4537	Norway
LF4539-4607	Sweden
LF4610-4827	Spain
LF4831-4887	Portugal
LF4901-5047	Switzerland
LF5051-5627	Turkey and the Baltic states

Subclass LG

LG21-961	Individual institutions
LG21-395	Asia
LG401-681	Africa
LG690	Indian Ocean islands
LG715-720	Australia
LG741-745	New Zealand
LG961	Pacific islands

Subclass LH

LH1-9	College and school magazines and papers

Subclass LJ

LJ3-165	Student fraternities and societies, United States

Subclass LT

LT6-501	Textbooks

Class here textbooks covering several subjects.

For textbooks on particular subjects, see the subject in B-Z

CLASS M - MUSIC

Subclass M

Music
  Vocal music
   Sacred vocal music - Continued

M2010-2017.6	Services
M2018-2019.5	Duets, trios, etc. for solo voices
M2020-2036	Choruses, cantatas, etc.
M2060-2101.5	Choruses, part-songs, etc., with accompaniment of keyboard or other solo instrument, or unaccompanied
M2102-2114.8	Songs
M2115-2146	Hymnals. Hymn collections
M2147-2188	Liturgy and ritual
M2190-2196	Sacred vocal music for children
M2198-2199	Gospel, revival, temperance, etc. songs
M5000	Unidentified compositions

Subclass ML

ML1-3930	Literature on music
ML112.8-158.8	Bibliography
ML113-118	International
ML120	National
ML132	Graded lists. By medium
ML135	Manuscripts
ML136-158	Catalogs. Discography
ML158.4-158.6	Video recordings
ML158.8	Computer software
ML159-3775	History and criticism
ML162-197	Special periods
ML162-169	Ancient
ML169.8-190	Medieval. Renaissance
ML193-197	1601-
ML198-360	By region or country
ML198-239	America
ML240-325	Europe
ML330-345	Asia
ML348	Arab countries
ML350	Africa
ML360	Australia, Oceania
ML385-429	Biography
ML430-455	Composition
ML459-1380	Instruments and instrumental music
ML465-471	By period
ML475-547	By region or country
ML475-486	America
ML489-522	Europe
ML525-541	Asia
ML544	Africa
ML547	Australia, Oceania
ML549-1093	Instruments
ML549.8-649	Organ
ML649.8-747	Piano, clavichord, harpsichord, etc.
ML749.5-927	Bowed string instruments

Subclass MT

Musical instruction and study - Continued

CLASS N - FINE ARTS

Subclass N

N1-9165	Visual arts
N400-3990	Art museums, galleries, etc.
N4390-5098	Exhibitions
N5198-5299	Private collections and collectors
N5300-7418	History
N7420-7525.8	General works
N7560-8266	Special subjects of art
N8350-8356	Art as a profession. Artists
N8510-8553	Art studios, materials, etc.
N8554-8585	Examination and conservation of works of art
N8600-8675	Economics of art
N8700-9165	Art and the state. Public art

Subclass NA

NA1-9428	Architecture
NA100-130	Architecture and the state
NA190-1555.5	History
NA2599.5-2599.9	Architectural criticism
NA2695-2793	Architectural drawing and design
NA2835-4050	Details and decoration
NA4100-8480	Special classes of buildings
NA4100-4145	Classed by material
NA4150-4160	Classed by form
NA4170-8480	Classed by use
NA4170-7010	Public buildings
NA4590-5621	Religious architecture
NA7100-7884	Domestic architecture. Houses. Dwellings
NA7910-8125	Clubhouses, guild houses, etc.
NA8200-8260	Farm architecture
NA8300-8480	Outbuildings, gates, fences, etc.
NA9000-9428	Aesthetics of cities. City planning and beautifying

Subclass NB

NB1-1952	Sculpture
NB1-50	General
NB60-1115	History
	Including collective biography
NB1120-1133	Study and teaching
NB1134-1134.4	Competitions
NB1135-1150	General works
NB1160-1195	Designs and technique
NB1199-1200	Restoration of sculptures
NB1203-1270	Special materials
NB1272-1291	Mobiles, color, sculpture gardens, etc.
NB1293-1895	Special forms

Subclass NE

NE1-3002	Print media
NE1-978	Printmaking and engraving
NE1-90	General
NE218-310	Engraved portraits. Self-portraits
NE380	Conservation and restoration of prints
NE390-395	Collected works
NE400-773	History of printmaking
NE830-898	General works
NE951-962	Special subjects
NE965-965.3	Tradesmen's cards
NE970-973	Study and teaching
NE975-975.4	Competitions
NE977-978	Equipment
NE1000-1352	Wood engraving
NE1000-1027	General
NE1030-1196.3	History
NE1220-1233	General works
NE1310-1326.5	Japanese prints
NE1330-1336	Linoleum block prints
NE1340	Fish prints
NE1344-1345	Potato prints
NE1350-1352	Other materials used in relief printing
NE1400-1879	Metal engraving
NE1400-1422	General
NE1620-1630	General works
NE1634-1749	History
NE1750-1775	Copper engraving
NE1850-1879	Color prints
NE1940-2232.5	Etching and aquatint
NE1940-1975	General
NE1980-2055.5	History
NE2120-2140	General works
NE2141-2149	Special subjects
NE2220-2225	Dry point
NE2236-2240.6	Serigraphy
NE2242-2246	Monotype (Printmaking)
NE2250-2570	Lithography
NE2685-2685.8	Lumiprints
NE2690	Engraving on glass
NE2800-2880	Printing of engravings
NE3000-3002	Copying art. Copying machine art

Subclass NK

NK1-9955	Decorative arts
NK1-570	General
NK600-806	History
NK1135-1149.5	Arts and crafts movement
NK1160-1590	Decoration and ornament. Design

	Decorative arts
	Decoration and ornament. Design - Continued
NK1175-1496.3	History
NK1505-1535	General works
NK1548-1590	Special subjects for design
NK1648-1678	Religious art
NK1700-2195	Interior decoration. House decoration
NK1700-2138	General. History, etc.
	Including special rooms
NK2140-2180	Decorative painting
NK2190-2192	Church decoration
NK2200-2750	Furniture
NK2775-2898	Rugs and carpets
NK2975-3049	Tapestries
NK3175-3296.3	Upholstery. Drapery
NK3375-3496.3	Wallpapers
NK3600-9955	Other arts and art industries
NK3700-4695	Ceramics
NK4700-4890	Costume
NK5100-5440	Glass
NK5500-6060	Glyptic arts
NK6400-8459	Metalwork
NK8800-9505.5	Textiles
NK9600-9955	Woodwork

Subclass NX

NX1-820	Arts in general
NX1-260	General
NX280-410	Study and teaching. Research
NX411-415	Competitions
NX420-430	Exhibitions
NX440-632	History of the arts
NX650-694	Special subjects, characters, persons, religious arts, etc.
NX700-750	Patronage of the arts
NX760-770	Administration of the arts
NX775-777	Voluntarism in the arts
NX798-820	Arts centers and facilities

CLASS P - LANGUAGE AND LITERATURE

Subclass P

P1-1091	Philology. Linguistics
P87-96	Communication. Mass media
P98-98.5	Computational linguistics. Natural language processing
P99-99.4	Semiotics
P99.5-99.6	Nonverbal communication
P101-410	Language. Linguistic theory. Comparative grammar
P118-118.7	Language acquisition
P121-149	Science of language (Linguistics)
P201-299	Comparative grammar
P301-301.5	Style. Composition. Rhetoric
P302-302.87	Discourse analysis
P306-310	Translating and interpreting
P321-324.5	Etymology
P325-325.5	Semantics
P326-326.5	Lexicology
P327-327.5	Lexicography
P375-381	Linguistic geography
P501-769	Indo-European (Indo-Germanic) philology
P901-1091	Extinct ancient or medieval languages

Subclass PA

PA1-199	Classical philology
PA227-895	Greek philology and language
PA1000-1177	Medieval and modern Greek language
PA2001-2915	Latin philology and language
PA3001-3043	Classical literature
PA3051-4505	Greek literature
PA3051-3285	Literary history
PA3300-3516	Collections
PA3520-3564	Criticism, interpretation, etc.
PA3601-3681	Translations
PA3818-4505	Individual authors
PA5000-5660	Byzantine and modern Greek literature
PA5301-5637	Individual authors
PA6001-6971	Roman literature
PA6001-6095.5	Literary history
PA6101-6140	Collections
PA6141-6144	Criticism, interpretation, etc.
PA6155-6191	Translations
PA6202-6971	Individual authors
PA8001-8595	Medieval and modern Latin literature
PA8200-8595	Individual authors

Subclass PB

PB1-3029	Modern languages. Celtic languages
PB1-431	General
PB1001-3029	Celtic languages and literature
PB1101-1200	Goidelic. Gaelic
PB1201-1449	Irish
PB1501-1709	Gaelic (Scottish Gaelic, Erse)
PB1801-1867	Manx
PB1950	Pict
PB2001-3029	Brittanic group
PB2101-2499	Welsh. Cymric
PB2501-2621	Cornish
PB2801-2932	Breton. Armorican
PB3001-3029	Gaulish

Subclass PC

PC1-5498	Romanic
PC1-400	General
PC601-872	Romanian
PC901-986	Raeto-Romance
	Including Romansh
PC1001-1977	Italian
PC1981-1984	Sardinian
PC2001-3761	French
PC2700-3680	Dialects. Provincialisms
PC2813-2896	Old French
PC3201-3366	Provencal (Old)
PC3371-3420.5	Modern patois of South France
PC3420.8-3495	Langue d'oc dialects
PC3721-3761	Slang. Argot
PC3801-3976	Catalan
PC4001-4977	Spanish
PC5001-5498	Portuguese

Subclass PD

PD1-7159	Germanic
PD1-777	General
PD1001-1350	Old Germanic dialects
PD1101-1211	Gothic
PD1501-5929	North Germanic. Scandinavian
PD2201-2392	Old Norse. Old Icelandic and Old Norwegian
PD2401-2489	Modern Icelandic
PD2483-2489	Old Norse dialects
PD2571-2999	Norwegian
PD3001-3929	Danish
PD5001-5929	Swedish

Subclass PE

PE1-3729	English
PE101-299	Anglo-Saxon. Old English
PE501-688	Middle English
PE828-896	Early Modern English
PE1001-1693	Modern English
PE1700-3602	Dialects. Provincialisms, etc.
PE3701-3729	Slang. Argot, etc.

Subclass PF

PF1-5999	West Germanic
PF1-979	Dutch
PF1001-1184	Flemish
PF1401-1541	Friesian
PF3001-5999	German
PF3801-3991	Old High German
PF3992-4010	Old Saxon
PF4043-4339	Middle High German
PF4514-4595	Early Modern German
PF5000-5951	Dialects. Provincialism, etc.
PF5971-5999	Slang. Argot, etc.

Subclass PG

PG1-9665	Slavic. Baltic. Albanian
PG1-7948	Slavic
PG1-499	Slavic philology and languages (General)
PG500-585	Slavic literature (General)
PG601-716	Church Slavic
PG801-1146	Bulgarian
PG1151-1199	Macedonian
PG1201-1696	Serbo-Croatian
PG1801-1962	Slovenian
PG2001-2826	Russian language
PG2830-2847	Belarusian
PG2900-3550	Russian literature
PG2900-3190	History and criticism
PG3199-3299	Collections
PG3300-3490	Individual authors and works
PG3300-3308	Early to 1700
PG3310-3319	18th century
PG3320-3447	1800-1870
PG3450-3470	1870-1917
PG3475-3476	1917-1960
PG3477-3490	1961-2000
PG3491.2-3493.96	2001-
PG3500-3505	Provincial, local, etc.

	Slavic. Baltic. Albanian
	Slavic
	Russian literature - Continued
PG3515-3550	Outside the Russian Federation
PG3801-3987	Ukrainian
PG3990	Carpatho-Rusyn
PG4001-5146	Czech
PG5201-5546	Slovak
PG5631-5689	Sorbian (Wendic)
PG6001-7446	Polish
PG7900-7925	Other Slavic dialects
PG8001-9146	Baltic
PG8201-8208	Old Prussian
PG8501-8772	Lithuanian
PG8801-9146	Latvian
PG9501-9665	Albanian

Subclass PH

PH1-5490	Uralic. Basque
PH1-87	General
PH91-98.5	Finnic. Baltic-Finnic
PH101-405	Finnish
PH501-1109	Other Finnic languages and dialects
PH501-509	Karelian
PH521-529	Olonets
PH531-539	Ludic
PH541-549	Veps
PH551-559	Ingrian
PH561-569	Votic
PH581-589	Livonian
PH601-671	Estonian
PH701-735	Lapp
PH751-785	Mordvin
PH801-836	Mari
PH1001-1079	Permic
PH1101-1109	Udmurt
PH1201-1409	Ugric languages
PH2001-3445	Hungarian
PH3801-3820	Samoyedic languages
PH5001-5490	Basque

Subclass PJ

PJ1-9348	Oriental philology and literature
PJ1-489	General
PJ1-187	Languages
PJ306-489	Literature

	Oriental philology and literature
	Arabic
	Language - Continued
PJ6950-7144	South Arabian
PJ6950-6981	Ancient
PJ7051-7144	Modern
PJ7501-8517	Arabic literature
PJ7695.8-7876	Individual authors or works
PJ8991-9293	Ethiopian languages
PJ9001-9101	Ethiopic (Geez)
PJ9201-9269	Amharic

Subclass PK

PK1-9201	Indo-Iranian philology and literature
PK1-85	General
PK101-2899	Indo-Aryan languages
PK101-185	General
PK207-379	Vedic
PK401-976	Sanskrit
PK1001-1095	Pali
PK1201-1409	Prakrit
PK1421-1429	Apabhramsa
PK1471-1490	Middle Indo-Aryan dialects
PK1501-2899	Modern Indo-Aryan languages
PK1550-2899	Particular languages and dialects
PK1550-1569	Assamese
PK1651-1799	Bengali
PK1801-1831	Bihārī
PK1841-1859	Gujarati
PK1931-2212	Hindī, Urdū, Hindustānī languages and literatures
PK1931-1970	Hindī language
PK1971-1979	Urdū language
PK1981-2000	Hindustānī language
PK2030-2142	Hindī, Hindustānī literatures
PK2151-2212	Urdū literature
PK2261-2270	Lahnda
PK2351-2418	Marāthī
PK2461-2479	Mārwārī
PK2561-2579.5	Oriyā (Uriyā)
PK2591-2610	Pahārī
PK2631-2659	Pañjābī
PK2701-2708.9	Rājasthānī
PK2781-2790	Sīndhī
PK2801-2891	Sinhalese (Singhalese)
PK2892-2892.95	Siraiki
PK2896-2899	Romany (Gipsy, Gypsy)

PK2901-5471	Indo-Aryan literature
PK2902-2979	General
PK3591-4485	Sanskrit
PK3791-3799	Individual authors and works
PK4471-4485	Translations
PK4501-4681	Pali literature
PK4990-5046	Prakrit literature
PK5401-5471	Modern Indo-Aryan literature
PK6001-6996	Iranian philology and literature
PK6001-6099	General
PK6102-6118	Avestan
PK6121-6129	Old Persian
PK6135-6199.5	Middle Iranian languages. Pahlavi
PK6201-6562.36	New Persian
PK6201-6399	Language
PK6400-6599.7	Literature
PK6450.9-6562.36	Individual authors or works
PK6701-6820	Afghan (Pashtō, Pushto, Pushtu, etc.)
PK7001-7075	Dardic (Pisacha)
PK7021-7037	Kāshmīrī
PK7040-7045	Kōhistānī
PK7050-7065	Nuristani (Kāfir) group
PK7070	Khōwār
PK7075	Phalura
PK8001-8835	Armenian
PK8001-8451	Language
PK8501-8835	Literature
PK9001-9201	Caucasian languages
PK9101-9169	Georgian

Subclass PL

PL1-8844	Languages of Eastern Asia, Africa, Oceania
PL1-481	Ural-Altaic languages
PL21-396	Turkic languages
PL400-431	Mongolian languages
PL450-481	Tungus Manchu languages
PL490-495	Far Eastern languages and literature
PL501-889	Japanese language and literature
PL501-699	Japanese language
PL700-889	Japanese literature
PL700-751.5	History and criticism
PL752-783	Collections
PL784-867	Individual authors and works
PL885-889	Local literature
PL901-998	Korean language and literature
PL901-949	Korean language
PL950-998	Korean literature
PL950.2-969.5	History and criticism

PL969.8-985	Collections
PL986-994.98	Individual authors and works
PL997-998	Local literature
PL1001-3208	Chinese language and literature
PL1001-1960	Chinese language
PL2250-3208	Chinese literature
PL2250-2443	History and criticism
PL2450-2659	Collections
PL2661-2979	Individual authors and works
PL3030-3208	Provincial, local, colonial, etc.
PL3301-3311	Non-Chinese languages of China
PL3501-3509	Non-Aryan languages of India and Southeastern Asia in general
PL3512	Malaysian literature
PL3515	Singapore literature
PL3518	Languages of the Montagnards
PL3521-4001	Sino-Tibetan languages
PL3551-4001	Tibeto-Burman languages
PL3561-3801	Tibeto-Himalayan languages
PL3601-3775	Tibetan
PL3781-3801	Himalayan languages
PL3851-4001	Assam and Burma
PL4051-4054	Karen languages
PL4070-4074	Miao-Yao languages
PL4281-4587	Austroasiatic languages
PL4301-4470	Mon-Khmer (Mon-Anam) languages
PL4371-4379	Vietnamese. Annamese
PL4423-4470	Bru, Chrau, Khasi, Muong, etc.
PL4471-4471.5	Nicobarese
PL4490-4498	Chamic languages
PL4501-4587	Munda languages (Kolarian languages)
PL4601-4797	Dravidian languages
PL5001-7511	Languages of Oceania
PL5001-7101	Austronesian, Papuan, and Australian languages
PL5051-5497	Malayan (Indonesian) languages
PL5501-6135	Philippine languages
PL6145-6167	Taiwan languages
PL6191-6341	Micronesian and Melanesian languages
PL6401-6551	Polynesian languages
PL6601-6621	Papuan languages
PL7001-7101	Australian languages
PL8000-8844	African languages and literature
PL8000-8009	Languages
PL8009.5-8014	Literature
PL8015-8021	Languages. By region or country
PL8024-8027	Special families of languages
PL8035-8844	Special languages (alphabetically)

Subclass PM

PM1-9021	Hyperborean, Indian, and artificial languages
PM1-94	Hperborean languages of Arctic Asia and America
PM101-2711	American languages (Aboriginal)
PM231-355	American languages of British North America
PM421-501	American languages of the United States (and Mexico)
PM549-2711	Special languages of the United States and Canada
PM3001-4566	Languages of Mexico and Central America
PM5001-7356	Languages of South America and the West Indies
PM7801-7895	Mixed languages
PM7831-7875	Creole languages
PM8001-8995	Artificial languages--Universal languages
PM8201-8298	Esperanto
PM8999	Picture languages
PM9001-9021	Secret languages

Subclass PN

PN1-6790	Literature (General)
PN80-99	Criticism
PN101-245	Authorship
PN441-1009.5	Literary history
PN597-605	Special relations, movements, and currents of literature
PN610-779	By period
PN611-649	Ancient
PN661-694	Medieval (to 1500)
PN695-779	Modern
PN715-749	Renaissance (1500-1700)
PN801-820	Romance literature
PN821-840	Germanic literature
PN841	Black literature (General)
PN842	Jewish literature in various languages
PN851-883	Comparative literature
PN1008.2-1009.5	Juvenile literature
PN1010-1525	Poetry
PN1031-1049	Theory, philosophy, relations, etc.
PN1065-1085	Relations to, and treatment of, special subjects
PN1110-1279	History and criticism
PN1301-1333	Epic poetry
PN1341-1347	Folk poetry
PN1351-1389	Lyric poetry
PN1530	The monologue
PN1551	The dialogue
PN1560-1590	The performing arts. Show business
PN1600-3307	Drama
PN1635-1650	Relation to, and treatment of, special subjects
PN1660-1693	Technique of dramatic composition
PN1720-1861	History
PN1865-1988	Special types

Drama - Continued

PN1990-1992.92	Broadcasting
PN1991-1991.9	Radio broadcasts
PN1992-1992.92	Television broadcasts
PN1992.93-19 92.95	Nonbroadcast video recordings
PN1993-1999	Motion pictures
PN1997-1997.85	Plays, scenarios, etc.
PN2000-3307	Dramatic representation. The theater
PN2131-2193	By period
PN2219.3-3030	Special regions or countries
PN3311-3503	Prose. Prose fiction
PN4001-4355	Oratory. Elocution, etc.
PN4390	Diaries
PN4400	Letters (Literary history)
PN4500	Essays (Literary history)
PN4699-5650	Journalism. The periodical press, etc.
PN4735-4748	Relation to the state. Government and the press. Liberty of the press
PN4775-4784	Technique. Practical journalism
PN4825-4830	Amateur journalism
PN4832-4836	Magazines and other periodicals
PN4840-5648	By region or country
PN6010-6790	Collections of general literature
PN6066-6069	Special classes of authors
PN6080-6095	Quotations
PN6099-6110	Poetry
PN6110.5-6120	Drama
PN6120.15-6120.95	Fiction
PN6121-6129	Orations
PN6130-6140	Letters
PN6141-6145	Essays
PN6146.5-6231	Wit and humor
PN6157-6222	By region or country
PN6233-6238	Anacreontic literature
PN6244-6246	Literary extracts. Commonplace books
PN6249-6258	Ana
PN6259-6268	Anecdotes. Table talk
PN6269-6278	Aphorisms. Apothegms
PN6279-6288	Epigrams
PN6288.5-6298	Epitaphs
PN6299-6308	Maxims
PN6309-6318	Mottoes
PN6319-6328	Sayings, bon mots, etc.
PN6329-6338	Thoughts
PN6340-6348	Toasts
PN6348.5-6358	Emblems, devices
PN6361	Paradoxes
PN6366-6377	Riddles, acrostics, charades, conundrums, etc.
PN6400-6525	Proverbs
PN6700-6790	Comic books, strips, etc.

Subclass PQ

PQ1-3999	French literature	
PQ1-771	History and criticism	
PQ1-150	General	
PQ151-221	Medieval. Old French	
PQ226-310	Modern	
PQ400-491	Poetry	
PQ500-591	Drama	
PQ601-771	Prose and prose fiction	
PQ845	Juvenile literature	
PQ1100-1297	Collections	
PQ1300-1595	Old French literature	
	To ca. 1500/1550	
PQ1300-1391	Collections	
	Individual authors and works	
PQ1411-1545	To 1350/1400	
PQ1551-1595	(14th-) 15th century (to ca. 1525)	
PQ1600-2726	Modern literature	
	Individual authors	
PQ1600-1709	16th century	
PQ1710-1935	17th century	
PQ1947-2147	18th century	
PQ2149-2551	19th century	
PQ2600-2651	1900-1960	
PQ2660-2686	1961-2000	
PQ2700-2726	2001-	
PQ3800-3999	Provincial, local, colonial, etc.	
PQ4001-5999	Italian literature	
PQ4001-4199.5	History and criticism	
PQ4001-4063	General	
PQ4064-4075	Early to 1500	
PQ4077-4088	Modern	
PQ4091-4130	Poetry	
PQ4133-4160	Drama	
PQ4161-4185	Prose	
PQ4199.5	Juvenile literature (General)	
PQ4201-4263	Collections	
PQ4265-4556	Individual authors and works to 1400	
PQ4561-4664	Individual authors, 1400-1700	
PQ4675-4734	Individual authors, 1701-1900	
PQ4800-4851	Individual authors, 1900-1960	
PQ4860-4886	Individual authors, 1961-2000	
PQ4900-4926	Individual authors, 2001-	
PQ5901-5999	Regional, provincial, local, etc.	
PQ6001-8929	Spanish literature	
PQ6001-6168	History and criticism	
PQ6001-6056	General	
PQ6056	Moorish-Spanish literature	
PQ6058-6060	Early to 1500	
PQ6063-6073	Modern	

	Spanish literature
	History and criticism - Continued
PQ6075-6098	Poetry
PQ6098.7-6129	Drama
PQ6131-6153	Prose
PQ6168	Juvenile literature (General)
PQ6170-6269	Collections
PQ6271-6498	Individual authors and works to 1700
PQ6500-6576	Individual authors, 1700-ca. 1868
PQ6600-6647	Individual authors, 1868-1960
PQ6650-6676	Individual authors, 1961-2000
PQ6700-6726	Individual authors, 2001-
PQ7000-8929	Provincial, local, colonial, etc.
PQ7081-8560	Spanish America
PQ9000-9999	Portuguese literature
PQ9000-9129	History and criticism
PQ9000-9034	General
PQ9035-9055	Special periods
PQ9061-9081	Poetry
PQ9083-9095	Drama
PQ9097-9119	Prose
PQ9129	Juvenile literature (General)
PQ9131-9188	Collections
PQ9189	Individual authors and works to 1500
PQ9191-9255	Individual authors and works, 1500-1700
PQ9261	Individual authors, 1701-1960
PQ9262-9288	Individual authors, 1961-2000
PQ9300-9326	Individual authors, 2001-
PQ9400-9999	Provincial, local, colonial, etc.
PQ9500-9698.436	Brazil

Subclass PR

PR1-9680	English literature
PR1-56	Literary history and criticism
PR57-78	Criticism
PR111-116	Women authors
PR125-138	Relations to other literatures and countries
PR161-478	By period
PR171-236	Anglo-Saxon (Beginnings through 1066)
PR251-369	Medieval. Middle English (1066-1500)
PR401-478	Modern
PR421-428	Elizabethan era (1550-1640)
PR431-438	17th century
PR441-448	18th century
PR451-468	19th century
PR471-478	20th century
PR500-611	Poetry
PR521-611	By period

English literature - Continued

PR621-739	Drama
PR641-739	By period
PR750-885	Prose
PR767-808	By period
PR821-885	Prose fiction. The novel
PR901-907	Oratory
PR908	Diaries
PR911-917	Letters
PR921-927	Essays
PR931-937	Wit and humor
PR1098-1369	Collections of English literature
PR1490-1799	Anglo-Saxon literature
PR1803-2165	Anglo-Norman period. Early English. Middle English
PR2199-3195	English renaissance (1500-1640)
PR3291-3785	17th and 18th centuries (1640-1770)
PR3991-5990	19th century, 1770/1800-1890/1900
PR6000-6049	1900-1960
PR6050-6076	1961-2000
PR6100-6126	2001-
PR8309-9680	English literature: Provincial, local, etc.

Subclass PS

PS1-3576	American literature
PS126-138	Biography, memoirs, letters, etc.
PS147-152	Women authors
PS163-173	Treatment of special subjects, classes
PS185-228	By period
PS241-286	Special regions, states, etc.
PS301-325	Poetry
PS330-352	Drama
PS360-379	Prose
PS400-408	Oratory
PS409	Diaries
PS410-418	Letters
PS420-428	Essays
PS430-438	Wit and humor. Satire
PS490	Juvenile literature (General)
PS501-688	Collections of American literature
PS700-3626	Individual authors
PS700-893	Colonial period (17th and 18th centuries)
PS991-3369	19th century
PS3500-3549	1900-1960
PS3550-3576	1961-2000
PS3600-3626	2001-
PS(8001-8599)	Canadian literature (alternate used by National Library of Canada)

Subclass PT

PT1-4897	German literature
PT1-80	Literary history and criticism
PT83-871	History of German literature
PT175-230	Medieval
PT236-405	Modern
PT500-597	Poetry
PT605-709	Drama
PT711-871	Prose
PT1100-1479	Collections
PT1501-2728	Individual authors or works
PT1501-1695	Middle High German, ca. 1050-1450/1500
PT1701-1797	1500-ca. 1700
PT1799-2592	1700-ca. 1860/70
PT1891-2239	Goethe
PT2600-2653	1860/70-1960
PT2660-2688	1961-2000
PT2700-2728	2001-
PT3701-3971	Provincial, local, colonial, etc.
PT3701-3746	East Germany
PT4801-4897	Low German literature
PT5001-5980	Dutch literature
PT5001-5348	Literary history and criticism
PT5001-5112	General
PT5121-5185	Special periods
PT5201-5243	Poetry
PT5250-5295	Drama
PT5300-5348	Prose
PT5398	Juvenile literature (General)
PT5400-5547	Collections
PT5555-5882.36	Individual authors or works
PT5555-5595	Medieval
PT5600-5739	16th-18th centuries
PT5800-5880	1800-1960
PT5881-5881.36	1961-2000
PT5882-5882.36	2001-
PT5901-5980	Provincial, local, foreign
PT6000-6467.36	Flemish literature since 1830
PT6000-6199	Literary history and criticism
PT6250	Juvenile literature (General)
PT6300-6397	Collections
PT6400-6467.36	Individual authors or works
PT6500-6593.36	Afrikaans literature
PT6500-6530	Literary history and criticism
PT6550-6575	Collections
PT6580	Local
PT6590-6593.36	Individual authors or works
PT7001-7099	Scandinavian literature

PT7101-7338	Old Norse literature: Old Icelandic and Old Norwegian
PT7101-7211	Literary history and criticism
PT7170-7176	Poetry
PT7177-7211	Prose
PT7181-7193	Sagas
PT7195-7211	Scientific and learned literature
PT7220-7262.5	Collections
PT7230-7252	Poetry
PT7255-7262.5	Prose
PT7261-7262.5	Sagas
PT7263-7296	Individual sagas and historical works
PT7298-7309	Religious works
PT7312-7318	Scientific and learned literature
PT7326-7338	Individual authors or works before 1540
PT7351-7550	Modern Icelandic literature
PT7351-7418	Literary history and criticism
PT7442	Juvenile literature (General)
PT7450-7495	Collections
PT7500-7513	Individual authors or works
PT7500-7501	16th-18th centuries
PT7510-7511	19th-20th centuries
PT7512-7513	21st century
PT7520-7550	Provincial, local, foreign
PT7581-7599	Faroese literature
PT7581-7592	Literary history and criticism
PT7593-7596.5	Collections
PT7597	Local
PT7598-7599	Individual authors or works
PT7601-8260	Danish literature
PT7601-7869	Literary history and criticism
PT7721-7762	Special periods
PT7770-7794	Poetry
PT7800-7832	Drama
PT7835-7869	Prose
PT7935	Juvenile literature (General)
PT7945-8046	Collections
PT8050-8177.36	Individual authors or works
PT8050	Medieval
PT8060-8098	16th-18th centuries
PT8100-8167	19th century
PT8174-8175	1900-1960
PT8176-8176.36	1961-2000
PT8177-8177.36	2001-
PT8205-8260	Provincial, local, foreign
PT8301-9155	Norwegian literature
PT8301-8574	Literary history and criticism
PT8425-8452	Special periods
PT8460-8489	Poetry
PT8500-8534	Drama
PT8540-8574	Prose
PT8640	Juvenile literature (General)

	Norwegian literature - Continued
PT8650-8733	Collections
PT8750-8952.36	Individual authors or works
PT8750-8775	16th-18th centuries
PT8800-8942	19th century
PT8949-8950	1900-1960
PT8951-8951.36	1961-2000
PT8952-8952.36	2001-
PT9000-9094	Landsmaal or New Norwegian
PT9064-9094	Individual authors
PT9100-9155	Provincial, local, foreign
PT9201-9999	Swedish literature
PT9201-9499	Literary history and criticism
PT9320-9370	Special periods
PT9375-9404	Poetry
PT9415-9449	Drama
PT9460-9499	Prose
PT9544	Juvenile literature (General)
PT9547-9639	Collections
PT9650-9877.36	Individual authors or works
PT9650-9651	Medieval
PT9674-9715	16th-18th centuries
PT9725-9850	19th century
PT9870-9875	1900-1960
PT9876-9876.36	1961-2000
PT9877-9877.36	2001-
PT9950-9999	Provincial, local, foreign

Subclass PZ

PZ1-90	Fiction and juvenile belles lettres
PZ5-90	Juvenile belles lettres

CLASS Q - SCIENCE

Subclass Q

Q1-390	Science (General)
Q1-295	General
Q300-390	Cybernetics
Q350-390	Information theory

Subclass QA

QA1-939	Mathematics
QA1-43	General
QA47-59	Tables
QA71-90	Instruments and machines
QA75-76.95	Calculating machines
QA75.5-76.95	Electronic computers. Computer science
QA76.75-76.765	Computer software
QA101-141.8	Elementary mathematics. Arithmetic
QA150-272.5	Algebra
QA273-280	Probabilities. Mathematical statistics
QA299.6-433	Analysis
QA440-699	Geometry. Trigonometry. Topology
QA801-939	Analytic mechanics

Subclass QB

QB1-991	Astronomy
QB1-139	General
QB140-237	Practical and spherical astronomy
QB275-343	Geodesy
QB349-421	Theoretical astronomy and celestial mechanics
QB455-456	Astrogeology
QB460-466	Astrophysics
QB468-480	Non-optical methods of astronomy
QB495-903	Descriptive astronomy
QB500.5-785	Solar system
QB799-903	Stars
QB980-991	Cosmogony. Cosmology

Subclass QC

QC1-999	Physics
QC1-75	General
QC81-114	Weights and measures
QC120-168.85	Descriptive and experimental mechanics
QC170-197	Atomic physics. Constitution and properties of matter
	Including molecular physics, relativity, quantum theory, and solid state physics

	Geology - Continued
QE701-760	Paleontology
QE760.8-899.2	Paleozoology
QE901-996.5	Paleobotany

Subclass QH

QH1-278.5	Natural history (General)
QH1-198	General
	Including nature conservation, geographical distribution
QH201-278.5	Microscopy
QH301-705.5	Biology (General)
QH359-425	Evolution
QH426-470	Genetics
QH471-489	Reproduction
QH501-531	Life
QH540-549.5	Ecology
QH573-671	Cytology
QH705-705.5	Economic biology

Subclass QK

QK1-989	Botany
QK1-474.5	General
	Including geographical distribution
QK474.8-495	Spermatophyta. Phanerogams
QK494-494.5	Gymnosperms
QK495	Angiosperms
QK504-635	Cryptogams
QK640-673	Plant anatomy
QK710-899	Plant physiology
QK900-989	Plant ecology

Subclass QL

QL1-991	Zoology
QL1-355	General
	Including geographical distribution
QL360-599.82	Invertebrates
QL461-599.82	Insects
QL605-739.8	Chordates. Vertebrates
QL614-639.8	Fishes
QL640-669.3	Reptiles and amphibians
QL671-699	Birds
QL700-739.8	Mammals
QL750-795	Animal behavior
QL791-795	Stories and anecdotes
QL799-799.5	Morphology
QL801-950.9	Anatomy
QL951-991	Embryology

Subclass QM

Subclass QP

Subclass QR

CLASS R - MEDICINE

Subclass R

R5-920	Medicine (General)
R131-687	History of medicine. Medical expeditions
R728-733	Practice of medicine. Medical practice economics
R735-854	Medical education. Medical schools. Research
R864	Medical records
R895-920	Medical physics. Medical radiology. Nuclear medicine

Subclass RA

RA1-1270	Public aspects of medicine
RA1-418.5	Medicine and the state
RA396	Regulation of medical education. Licensure
RA398	Registration of physicians, pharmacists, etc.
RA399	Regulation of medical practice. Evaluation and quality control of medical care. Medical audit
RA405	Death certification
RA407-409.5	Health status indicators. Medical statistics and surveys
RA410-410.9	Medical economics. Economics of medical care. Employment
RA411-415	Provisions for personal medical care. Medical care plans
RA418-418.5	Medicine and society. Social medicine. Medical sociology
RA421-790.95	Public health. Hygiene. Preventive medicine
RA565-600	Environmental health
	Including sewage disposal, air pollution, nuisances, water supply
RA601-602	Food and food supply in relation to public health
RA604-618	Parks, public baths, public carriers, buildings, etc.
RA619-637	Disposal of the dead. Undertaking. Burial. Cremation. Cemeteries
RA638	Immunity and immunization in relation to public health
RA639-642	Transmission of disease
RA643-645	Disease (Communicable and noninfectious) and public health
RA645.3-645.37	Home health care services
RA645.5-645.9	Emergency medical services
RA646-648.3	War and public health
RA648.5-767	Epidemics. Epidemiology. Quarantine. Disinfection
RA771-771.7	Rural health and hygiene. Rural health services
RA773-788	Personal health and hygiene
RA790-790.95	Mental health. Mental illness prevention
RA791-954	Medical geography. Climatology. Meteorology
RA960-1000.5	Medical centers. Hospitals. Dispensaries. Clinics
	Including ambulance service, nursing homes, hospices
RA1001-1171	Forensic medicine. Medical jurisprudence. Legal medicine
RA1190-1270	Toxicology. Poisons

Subclass RB

RB1-214	Pathology
RB24-33	Pathological anatomy and histology
RB37-56.5	Clinical pathology. Laboratory technique
RB127-150	Manifestations of disease
RB151-214	Theories of disease. Etiology. Pathogenesis

Subclass RC

RC31-1245	Internal medicine
RC49-52	Psychosomatic medicine
RC71-78.7	Examination. Diagnosis
RC78-78.5	Radiography. Roentgenography
RC81-82	Popular medicine
RC86-88.9	Medical emergencies. Critical care. Intensive care. First aid
RC91-103	Disease due to physical and chemical agents
RC109-216	Infectious and parasitic diseases
RC254-282	Neoplasms. Tumors. Oncology. Including cancer and carcinogens
RC306-320.5	Tuberculosis
RC321-571	Neurosciences. Biological psychiatry. Neuropsychiatry
RC346-429	Neurology. Diseases of the nervous system
RC423-429	Speech and language disorders
RC435-571	Psychiatry
RC475-489	Therapeutics. Psychotherapy
RC490-499	Hypnotism and hypnosis. Suggestion therapy
RC500-510	Psychoanalysis
RC512-569.5	Psychopathology
RC569.7-571	Mental retardation. Developmental disabilities
RC581-951	Specialties of internal medicine
RC581-607	Immunologic diseases. Allergy
RC620-627	Nutritional diseases. Deficiency diseases
RC627.5-632	Metabolic diseases
RC633-647.5	Diseases of the blood and blood-forming organs
RC648-665	Diseases of the endocrine glands. Clinical endocrinology
RC666-701	Diseases of the circulatory (Cardiovascular) system
RC705-779	Diseases of the respiratory system
RC799-869	Diseases of the digestive system. Gastroenterology
RC870-923	Diseases of the genitourinary system. Urology
RC924-924.5	Diseases of the connective tissues
RC925-935	Diseases of the musculoskeletal system
RC952-1245	Special situations and conditions
RC952-954.6	Geriatrics
RC955-962	Arctic medicine. Tropical medicine
RC963-969	Industrial medicine. Industrial hygiene
RC970-986	Military medicine. Naval medicine
RC1000-1020	Submarine medicine
RC1030-1160	Transportation medicine
	Including automotive, aviation, and space medicine
RC1200-1245	Sports medicine

Subclass RD

RD1-811	Surgery
RD1-31.7	General works
RD32-33.9	Operative surgery. Technique of surgical operations
RD49-52	Surgical therapeutics. Preoperative and postoperative care
RD57	Surgical pathology
RD58	Reparative processes after operations (Physiological)
RD59	Surgical shock. Traumatic shock
RD63-76	Operating rooms and theaters. Instruments, apparatus, and appliances
RD78.3-87.3	Anesthesiology
RD91-91.5	Asepsis and antisepsis. Sterilization (Operative)
RD92-97.8	Emergency surgery. Wounds and injuries
RD98-98.4	Surgical complications
RD99-99.35	Surgical nursing
RD101-104	Fractures (General)
RD118-120.5	Plastic surgery. Reparative surgery
RD120.6-129.8	Transplantation of organs, tissues, etc.
RD130	Prosthesis. Artificial organs
RD137-145	Surgery in childhood, adolescence, pregnancy, old age
RD151-498	Military and naval surgery
RD520-599.5	Surgery by region, system, or organ
RD651-678	Neoplasms. Tumors. Oncology
RD680-688	Diseases of the locomotor system (Surgical treatment)
RD701-811	Orthopedic surgery
RD792-811	Physical rehabilitation

Subclass RE

RE1-994	Ophthalmology
RE75-79	Examination. Diagnosis
RE80-87	Eye surgery
RE88	Ophthalmic nursing
RE89	Eye banks
RE91-912	Particular diseases of the eye
RE918-921	Color vision tests, charts, etc.
RE925-939	Refraction and errors of refraction and accommodation
RE939.2-981	Optometry. Opticians. Eyeglasses
RE986-988	Artificial eyes and other prostheses
RE991-992	Ocular therapeutics

Subclass RF

RF1-547	Otorhinolaryngology
RF110-320	Otology. Diseases of the ear
RF341-437	Rhinology. Diseases of the nose, accessory sinuses, and nasopharynx
RF460-547	Laryngology. Diseases of the throat

Subclass RG

RG1-991	Gynecology and obstetrics
RG104-104.7	Operative gynecology
RG133-137.6	Conception. Artificial insemination. Contraception
RG159-208	Functional and systemic disorders. Endocrine gynecology
RG211-483	Abnormalities and diseases of the female genital organs
RG484-485	Urogynecology and obstetric urology. Urogynecologic surgery
RG491-499	Diseases of the breast
RG500-991	Obstetrics
RG551-591	Pregnancy
RG600-650	The embryo and fetus
RG651-721	Labor. Parturition
RG725-791	Obstetric operations. Operative obstetrics
RG801-871	Puerperal state
RG940-991	Maternal care. Prenatal care services

Subclass RJ

RJ1-570	Pediatrics
RJ47.3-47.4	Genetic aspects
RJ50-51	Examination. Diagnosis
RJ52-53	Therapeutics
RJ59-60	Infant and neonatal morbidity and mortality
RJ91	Supposed prenatal influence. Prenatal culture. Stirpiculture
RJ101-103	Child health. Child health services
RJ125-145	Physiology of children and adolescents
RJ206-235	Nutrition and feeding of children and adolescents
RJ240	Immunization of children (General)
RJ242-243	Hospital care
RJ245-247	Nursing of children. Pediatric nursing
RJ250-250.3	Premature infants
RJ251-325	Newborn infants
	Including physiology, care, treatment, diseases
RJ370-550	Diseases of children and adolescents
RJ499-507	Mental disorders. Child psychiatry

Subclass RK

RK1-715	Dentistry
RK58-59.3	Practice of dentistry. Dental economics
RK60.7-60.8	Preventive dentistry
RK280	Oral and dental anatomy and physiology
RK301-493	Oral and dental medicine. Pathology. Diseases
RK501-519	Operative dentistry. Restorative dentistry
RK520-528	Orthodontics
RK529-535	Oral surgery
RK641-667	Prosthetic dentistry. Prosthodontics

Subclass RL

RL1-803	Dermatology
RL87-94	Care and hygiene
RL95	Pathological anatomy
RL110-120	Therapeutics
RL130-169	Diseases of the glands, hair, nails
RL201-331	Hyperemias, inflammations, and infections of the skin
RL391-489	Atrophies. Hypertrophies
RL675	Chronic ulcer of the skin. Bedsores
RL701-751	Diseases due to psychosomatic and nerve disorders. Dermatoneuroses
RL760-785	Diseases due to parasites
RL790	Pigmentations. Albinism
RL793	Congenital disorders of the skin. Nevi. Moles

Subclass RM

RM1-950	Therapeutics. Pharmacology
RM138	Drug prescribing
RM139	Prescription writing
RM146-146.7	Misuse of therapeutic drugs. Medication errors
RM147-180	Administration of drugs and other therapeutic agents
RM182-190	Other therapeutic procedures
	Including acupuncture, pneumatic aspiration, spinal puncture, pericardial puncture
RM214-258	Diet therapy. Dietary cookbooks
RM259	Vitamin therapy
RM260-263	Chemotherapy
RM265-267	Antibiotic therapy. Antibiotics
RM270-282	Immunotherapy. Serotherapy
RM283-298	Endocrinotherapy. Organotherapy
RM300-666	Drugs and their actions
RM671-671.5	Nonprescription drugs. Patent medicines
RM695-893	Physical medicine. Physical therapy
	Including massage, exercise, occupational therapy, hydrotherapy, phototherapy, radiotherapy, thermotherapy, electrotherapy
RM930-931	Rehabilitation therapy
RM950	Rehabilitation technology

Subclass RS

RS1-441	Pharmacy and materia medica
RS125-131.9	Formularies. Collected prescriptions
RS139-141.9	Pharmacopoeias
RS151.2-151.9	Dispensatories
RS153-441	Materia medica
RS160-167	Pharmacognosy. Pharmaceutical substances (Plant, animal, and inorganic)

	Pharmacy and materia medica
	Materia medica - Continued
RS189-190	Assay methods. Standardization. Analysis
RS192-199	Pharmaceutical technology
RS200-201	Pharmaceutical dosage forms
RS250-252	Commercial preparations. Patent medicines
RS355-356	Pharmaceutical supplies
RS400-431	Pharmaceutical chemistry
RS441	Microscopical examination of drugs

Subclass RT

RT1-120	Nursing
RT89-120	Specialties in nursing

Subclass RV

RV1-431	Botanic, Thomsonian, and eclectic medicine

Subclass RX

RX1-681	Homeopathy
RX211-581	Diseases, treatment, etc.
RX601-675	Materia medica and therapeutics

Subclass RZ

RZ201-999	Other systems of medicine
RZ201-275	Chiropractic
RZ301-397.5	Osteopathy
RZ399	Osteo-magnetics, neuropathy, etc., A-Z
RZ400-408	Mental healing
RZ409.7-999	Miscellaneous systems and treatments
	Including magnetotherapy, mesmerism, naturopathy, organomic medicine, phrenology, radiesthesia

Subclass S

S1-946.5	Agriculture (General)
S419-482	History
S530-559	Agricultural education
S560-571.5	Farm economics. Farm management. Agricultural mathematics
	Including production standards, record keeping, farmwork rates, marketing
S583-587.73	Agricultural chemistry. Agricultural chemicals
S588.4-589.6	Agricultural physics
	Including radioisotopes in agriculture
S589.7	Agricultural ecology (General)
S589.75-589.76	Agriculture and the environment
S589.8-589.87	Plant growing media. Potting soils
S590-599.9	Soils. Soil science
	Including soil surveys, soil chemistry, soil structure, soil-plant relationships
S600-600.7	Agricultural meteorology. Crops and climate
S602.5-604.37	Methods and systems of culture. Cropping systems
	Including fallowing, rotation of crops, plowing
S604.5-604.64	Agricultural conservation
S604.8-621.5	Melioration: Improvement, reclamation, fertilization, irrigation, etc., of lands
S605.5	Organic farming. Organiculture
S606-621.5	Special classes of lands and reclamation methods
	Including woodlands, burning of lands, deserts, saline environments, moors
S622-627	Soil conservation and protection
S631-667	Fertilizers and improvement of the soil
S671-760.5	Farm machinery and farm engineering
S770-790.3	Agricultural structures. Farm buildings
S900-946.5	Conservation of natural resources
	Including land conservation

Subclass SB

SB1-1110	Plant culture
SB39	Horticultural voyages, etc.
SB71-87	History
SB107-109	Economic botany
SB109.7-111	Methods for special areas
	Including cold regions, dry farming, tropical agriculture
SB112	Irrigation farming
SB113.2-118.46	Seeds. Seed technology
SB118.48-118.75	Nurseries. Nursery industry
SB119-124	Propagation
	Including breeding, selection, grafting, air layering
SB125	Training and pruning

SB126	Artificial light gardening
SB126.5-126.57	Hydroponics. Soilless agriculture
SB127	Forcing
SB128	Growth regulators
SB129-130	Harvesting, curing, storage
SB169-172.5	Tree crops
SB175-177	Food crops
SB183-317	Field crops
SB317.5-319.864	Horticulture. Horticultural crops
SB320-353.5	Vegetables
SB354-402	Fruit and fruit culture
SB381-386	Berries and small fruits
SB387-399	Grape culture. Viticulture
SB401	Nuts
SB403-450.87	Flowers and flower culture. Ornamental plants
SB406.7-406.83	Plant propagation
SB409-413	Culture of individual plants
SB414	Forcing
SB414.6-417	Greenhouses and greenhouse culture
SB418-418.4	Container gardening
SB419-419.3	Indoor gardening and houseplants
SB419.5	Roof gardening. Balcony gardening
SB421-439.8	Classes of plants
	Including annuals, climbers, ferns, lawns, perennials, shrubs
SB441-441.75	Flower shows. Exhibitions
SB442.5	Care and preparation of cut flowers and ornamental plants for market
SB442.8-443.4	Marketing. Cut flower industry. Florists
SB446-446.6	Horticultural service industry
SB447	Preservation and reproduction of flowers, fruits, etc.
SB447.5	Bonkei. Tray landscapes
SB449-450.87	Flower arrangement and decoration
SB450.9-467.8	Gardens and gardening
SB469-476	Landscape gardening. Landscape architecture
SB481-486	Parks and public reservations
SB599-990.5	Pests and diseases
SB608	Individual or types of plants or trees
SB610-615	Weeds, parasitic plants, etc.
SB617-618	Poisonous plants
SB621-795	Plant pathology
SB818-945	Economic entomology
SB950-990.5	Pest control and treatment of diseases. Plant protection
SB992-998	Economic zoology applied to crops. Agricultural zoology
	Including animals injurious and beneficial to plants

Subclass SD

SD1-669.5	Forestry
SD119	Voyages, etc.
SD131-247.5	History of forestry. Forest conditions
SD250-363.3	Forestry education
SD388	Forestry machinery and engineering
SD388.5	Tools and implements
SD389	Forest roads
SD390-390.43	Forest soils
SD390.5-390.7	Forest meteorology. Forest microclimatology
SD391-410.9	Sylviculture
SD411-428	Conservation and protection
	Including forest influences, damage by elements, fires, forest reserves
SD430-557	Exploitation and utilization
	Including timber trees, fuelwood, logging, transportation, valuation
SD561-669.5	Administration. Policy

Subclass SF

SF1-1100	Animal culture
SF41-55	History
SF84-84.64	Economic zoology
SF84.82-85.6	Rangelands. Range management. Grazing
SF87	Acclimatization
SF89	Transportation
SF91	Housing and environmental control
SF92	Equipment and supplies
SF94.5-99	Feeds and feeding. Animal nutrition
SF101-103.5	Brands and branding, and other means of identifying
SF105-109	Breeding and breeds
SF111-113	Cost, yield, and profit. Accounting
SF114-121	Exhibitions
SF170-180	Working animals
SF191-275	Cattle
SF221-250	Dairying
SF250.5-275	Dairy processing. Dairy products
SF277-360.4	Horses
SF294.2-297	Horse sports. Horse shows
SF304.5-307	Driving
SF308.5-310.5	Horsemanship. Riding
SF311-312	Draft horses
SF315-315.5	Ponies
SF321-359.7	Racing
SF360-360.4	Feral horses. Wild horses
SF361-361.73	Donkeys
SF362	Mules
SF371-379	Sheep. Wool

Subclass SH

Subclass SK

CLASS T - TECHNOLOGY

Subclass T

T1-995	Technology (General)
T11.95-12.5	Industrial directories
T55-55.3	Industrial safety. Industrial accident prevention
T55.4-60.8	Industrial engineering. Management engineering
T57-57.97	Applied mathematics. Quantitative methods
T57.6-57.97	Operations research. Systems analysis
T58.4	Managerial control systems
T58.5-58.64	Information technology
T58.6-58.62	Management information systems
T58.7-58.8	Production capacity. Manufacturing capacity
T59-59.2	Standardization
T59.5	Automation
T59.7-59.77	Human engineering in industry. Man-machine systems
T60-60.8	Work measurement. Methods engineering
T61-173	Technical education. Technical schools
T173.2-174.5	Technological change
T175-178	Industrial research. Research and development
T201-342	Patents. Trademarks
T351-385	Mechanical drawing. Engineering graphics
T391-995	Exhibitions. Trade shows. World's fairs

Subclass TA

TA1-2040	Engineering (General). Civil engineering (General)
TA164	Bioengineering
TA165	Engineering instruments, meters, etc. Industrial instrumentation
TA166-167	Human engineering
TA168	Systems engineering
TA170-171	Environmental engineering
TA174	Engineering design
TA177.4-185	Engineering economy
TA190-194	Management of engineering works
TA197-198	Engineering meteorology
TA213-215	Engineering machinery, tools, and implements
TA329-348	Engineering mathematics. Engineering analysis
TA349-359	Mechanics of engineering. Applied mechanics
TA365-367	Acoustics in engineering. Acoustical engineering
TA401-492	Materials of engineering and construction. Mechanics of materials
TA495	Disasters and engineering
TA501-625	Surveying
TA630-695	Structural engineering (General)
TA703-712	Engineering geology. Rock mechanics. Soil mechanics. Underground construction
TA715-787	Earthwork. Foundations
TA800-820	Tunneling. Tunnels
TA1001-1280	Transportation engineering

Engineering (General). Civil engineering (General) - Continued

TA1501-1820	Applied optics. Photonics
TA2001-2040	Plasma engineering. Applied plasma dynamics

Subclass TC

TC1-978	Hydraulic engineering
TC160-181	Technical hydraulics
TC183-201	General preliminary operations. Dredging. Submarine building
TC203-380	Harbors and coast protective works. Coastal engineering. Lighthouses
TC401-506	River, lake, and water-supply engineering (General)
TC530-537	River protective works. Regulation. Flood control
TC540-558	Dams. Barrages
TC601-791	Canals and inland navigation. Waterways
TC801-978	Irrigation engineering. Reclamation of wasteland. Drainage
TC1501-1800	Ocean engineering

Subclass TD

TD1-1066	Environmental technology. Sanitary engineering
TD159-168	Municipal engineering
TD169-171.8	Environmental protection
TD172-193.5	Environmental pollution
TD194-195	Environmental effects of industries and plants
TD201-500	Water supply for domestic and industrial purposes
TD419-428	Water pollution
TD429.5-480.7	Water purification. Water treatment and conditioning. Saline water conversion
TD481-493	Water distribution systems
TD511-780	Sewage collection and disposal systems. Sewerage
TD783-812.5	Municipal refuse. Solid wastes
TD813-870	Street cleaning. Litter and its removal
TD878-894	Special types of environment
	Including soil pollution, air pollution, noise pollution
TD895-899	Industrial and factory sanitation
TD896-899	Industrial and factory wastes
TD920-934	Rural and farm sanitary engineering
TD940-949	Low temperature sanitary engineering
TD1020-1066	Hazardous substances and their disposal

Subclass TE

TE1-450	Highway engineering. Roads and pavements
TE175-176.5	Highway design. Interchanges and intersections
TE177-178.8	Roadside development. Landscaping
TE200-205	Materials for roadmaking
TE206-209.5	Location engineering
TE210-228.3	Construction details
	Including foundations, maintenance, equipment

TE250-278.8	Pavements and paved roads
TE279	Streets
TE279.5-298	Pedestrian facilities
TE280-295	Sidewalks. Footpaths. Flagging
TE298	Curbs. Curbstones

Subclass TF

TF1-1620	Railroad engineering and operation
TF200-320	Railway construction
TF340-499	Railway equipment and supplies
TF501-668	Railway operation and management
TF670-851	Local and light railways
TF840-851	Elevated railways and subways
TF855-1127	Electric railways
TF1300-1620	High speed ground transporation

Subclass TG

TG1-470	Bridge engineering

Subclass TH

TH1-9745	Building construction
TH845-895	Architectural engineering. Structural engineering of buildings
TH900-915	Construction equipment in building
TH1000-1725	Systems of building construction
	Including fireproof construction, concrete construction
TH2025-3000	Details in building design and construction
	Including walls, roofs
TH3301-3411	Maintenance and repair
TH4021-4977	Buildings: Construction with reference to use
	Including public buildings, dwellings
TH5011-5701	Construction by phase of the work (Building trades)
TH6014-6081	Environmental engineering of buildings. Sanitary engineering of buildings
TH6101-6887	Plumbing and pipefitting
TH7005-7699	Heating and ventilation. Air conditioning
TH7700-7975	Illumination. Lighting
TH8001-8581	Decoration and decorative furnishings
TH9025-9745	Protection of buildings
	Including protection from dampness, fire, burglary

Subclass TJ

TJ1-1570	Mechanical engineering and machinery
TJ163.13-163.25	Power resources
TJ163.26-163.5	Energy conservation
TJ170-179	Mechanics applied to machinery. Dynamics

TJ181-210	Mechanical movements
TJ210.2-211.47	Mechanical devices and figures. Automata. Ingenious mechanisms. Robots (General)
TJ212-225	Control engineering systems. Automatic machinery (General)
TJ227-240	Machine design and drawing
TJ241-254.7	Machine construction (General)
TJ255-265	Heat engines
TJ266-267.5	Turbines. Turbomachines (General)
TJ268-740	Steam engineering
TJ603-695	Locomotives
TJ751-805	Miscellaneous motors and engines
	Including gas, gasoline, diesel engines
TJ807-830	Renewable energy sources
TJ836-927	Hydraulic machinery
TJ940-940.5	Vacuum technology
TJ950-1030	Pneumatic machinery
TJ1040-1119	Machinery exclusive of prime movers
TJ1125-1345	Machine shops and machine shop practice
TJ1350-1418	Hoisting and conveying machinery
TJ1425-1475	Lifting and pressing machinery
TJ1480-1496	Agricultural machinery. Farm machinery
TJ1501-1519	Sewing machines

Subclass TK

TK1-9971	Electrical engineering. Electronics. Nuclear engineering
TK301-399	Electric meters
TK452-454.4	Electric apparatus and materials. Electric circuits. Electric networks
TK1001-1841	Production of electric energy or power. Powerplants. Central stations
TK2000-2891	Dynamoelectric machinery and auxiliaries
	Including generators, motors, transformers
TK2896-2985	Production of electricity by direct energy conversion
TK3001-3521	Distribution or transmission of electric power
TK4001-4102	Applications of electric power
TK4125-4399	Electric lighting
TK4601-4661	Electric heating
TK5101-6720	Telecommunication
	Including telegraphy, telephone, radio, radar, television
TK7800-8360	Electronics
TK7885-7895	Computer engineering. Computer hardware
TK8300-8360	Photoelectronic devices (General)
TK9001-9401	Nuclear engineering. Atomic power
TK9900-9971	Electricity for amateurs. Amateur constructors' manuals

Subclass TL

TL1-4050	Motor vehicles. Aeronautics. Astronautics
TL1-484	Motor vehicles. Cycles
TL500-777	Aeronautics. Aeronautical engineering
TL780-785.8	Rocket propulsion. Rockets
TL787-4050	Astronautics. Space travel

Subclass TN

TN1-997	Mining engineering. Metallurgy
TN263-271	Mineral deposits. Metallic ore deposits. Prospecting
TN275-325	Practical mining operations. Safety measures
TN331-347	Mine transportation, haulage and hoisting. Mining machinery
TN400-580	Ore deposits and mining of particular metals
TN600-799	Metallurgy
TN799.5-948	Nonmetallic minerals
TN950-997	Building and ornamental stones

Subclass TP

TP1-1185	Chemical technology
TP155-156	Chemical engineering
TP200-248	Chemicals: Manufacture, use, etc.
TP248.13-248.65	Biotechnology
TP250-261	Industrial electrochemistry
TP267.5-301	Explosives and pyrotechnics
TP315-360	Fuel
TP368-456	Food processing and manufacture
TP480-498	Low temperature engineering. Cryogenic engineering. Refrigeration
TP500-660	Fermentation industries. Beverages. Alcohol
TP670-699	Oils, fats, and waxes
TP690-692.5	Petroleum refining. Petroleum products
TP700-746	Illuminating industries (Nonelectric)
TP751-762	Gas industry
TP785-869	Clay industries. Ceramics. Glass
TP875-888	Cement industries
TP890-933	Textile bleaching, dyeing, printing, etc.
TP934-945	Paints, pigments, varnishes, etc.
TP1080-1185	Polymers and polymer manufacture

Subclass TR

TR1-1050	Photography
TR250-265	Cameras
TR287-500	Photographic processing. Darkroom technique
TR504-508	Transparencies. Diapositives
TR510-545	Color photography
TR550-581	Studio and laboratory
TR590-620	Lighting

CLASS U - MILITARY SCIENCE

Subclass U

U1-900	Military science (General)
U56-59	Army clubs
U150-155	Military planning
U161-163	Strategy
U164-167.5	Tactics
U168	Logistics
U250-255	Maneuvers (combined arms)
U260	Joint operations. Combined operations
U261	Amphibious warfare
U262	Commando tactics
U263-264.5	Atomic warfare. Atomic weapons
U300-305	Artillery and rifle ranges
U310-310.2	War games
U320-325	Physical training of soldiers
U400-714	Military education and training
U750-773	Military life, manners and customs, antiquities, etc.
U799-897	History of arms and armor

Subclass UA

UA10-997	Armies: Organization, distribution, military situation
UA21-885	By region or country
UA910-915	Mobilization
UA920-925	Plans for attack and defense
UA926-929	Civil defense
UA929.5-929.95	War damage in industry. Industrial defense
UA940-945	Military communication
UA950-979	Routes of travel. Distances
UA985-997	Military geography

Subclass UB

UB1-900	Military administration
UB160-165	Records, returns, muster rolls, etc.
UB170-175	Adjutant generals' offices
UB180-197	Civilian personnel departments
UB250-271	Intelligence
UB273-274	Sabotage
UB275-277	Psychological warfare. Propaganda
UB320-338	Enlistment, recruiting, etc.
UB340-345	Compulsory service. Conscription and exemption
UB356-369.5	Provision for veterans
UB370-375	Military pensions, etc.
UB380-385	Soldiers' and sailors' homes
UB407-409	Warrant officers. Noncommissioned officers
UB410-415	Officers
UB416-419	Minorities, women, etc. in armed forces

UB420-425	Furloughs
UB440-449.5	Retired military personnel

Subclass UC

UC10-780	Maintenance and transportation
UC20-258	Organization of the service. By region or country
UC260-267	Supplies and stores
UC270-360	Transportation
UC400-440	Barracks. Quarters. Camps
UC460-535	Clothing and equipment
UC540-585	Equipage. Field kits
UC600-695	Horses. Mules. Remount service
UC700-780	Subsistence

Subclass UD

UD1-495	Infantry
UD157-302	Tactics. Maneuvers. Drill regulations
UD320-325	Manual of arms
UD330-335	Firing. Military sharpshooting
UD340-345	Bayonet drill
UD380-425	Small arms. Swords, etc.
UD450-455	Mounted infantry
UD460-464	Mountain troops
UD470-475	Ski troops
UD480-485	Airborne troops. Parachute troops
UD490-495	Airmobile operations

Subclass UE

UE1-500	Cavalry. Armor
	Including horse cavalry, armored cavalry, mechanized cavalry
UE144-145	Horse cavalry
UE147	Armored cavalry
UE157-302	Tactics. Maneuvers. Drill regulations
UE420-425	Cavalry sword exercises
UE460-475	Horses

Subclass UF

UF1-910	Artillery
UF157-302	Tactics. Maneuvers. Drill regulations
UF400-405	Field artillery
UF450-455	Seacoast artillery
UF460-465	Siege artillery
UF470-475	Howitzer artillery. Mortar batteries
UF480-485	Garrison artillery
UF500-515	Weapons systems
UF520-537	Ordnance and small arms

CLASS V - NAVAL SCIENCE

Subclass V

V1-995	Naval science (General)
V25-55	History and antiquities of naval science
V66-69	Navy clubs
V160-165	Strategy
V167-178	Tactics
V200	Coast defense
V210-214.5	Submarine warfare
V390-395	Naval research
V396-396.5	Military oceanography
V399	Automation in the naval sciences
V400-695	Naval education
V720-743	Naval life, manners and customs, antiquities, etc.
V750-995	War vessels: Construction, armament, etc.

Subclass VA

VA10-750	Navies: Organization, distribution, naval situation
VA49-395	United States
VA400-750	Other regions or countries

Subclass VB

VB15-345	Naval administration
VB21-124	By region or country
VB170-187	Civil department
VB260-275	Enlisted personnel
VB307-309	Warrant officers
VB310-315	Officers
VB320-325	Minorities, women, etc. in navies

Subclass VC

VC10-580	Naval maintenance
VC20-258	Organization of service
VC260-268	Supplies and stores
VC270-279	Equipment of vessels, supplies, allowances, etc.
VC280-345	Clothing and equipment
VC350-410	Subsistence. Provisioning
VC412-425	Navy yards and stations. Shore facilities

Subclass VD

VD7-430	Naval seamen
VD21-124	By region or country
VD160-302	Drill regulations

	Naval seamen - Continued
VD330-335	Shooting
VD360-390	Small arms
VD400-405	Small boat service

Subclass VE

	Marines
VE7-500	
VE23-124	By region or country
VE160-302	Drill regulations
VE330-335	Shooting
VE360-390	Small arms
VE420-425	Barracks, quarters, etc.
VE430-435	Training camps

Subclass VF

	Naval ordnance
VF1-580	
VF21-124	By region or country
VF160-302	Ordnance instructions and drill books
VF310-315	Target practice
VF346-348	Naval weapons systems
VF350-375	Ordnance and arms (General)
VF390-510	Ordnance material (Ordnance proper)

Subclass VG

	Minor services of navies
VG20-2029	
VG20-25	Chaplains
VG50-55	Coast guard and coast signal service
VG70-85	Naval communication by telegraphy, telephone, etc.
VG90-95	Naval aviation
VG100-475	Medical service
VG500-505	Public relations. Press. War correspondents
VG2000-2005	Social work. Social welfare services
VG2020-2029	Recreation and information service

Subclass VK

	Navigation. Merchant marine
VK1-1661	
VK15-124	History, conditions, etc.
VK321-369.8	Harbors. Ports
VK381-397	Signaling
VK401-529	Study and teaching
VK549-572	Science of navigation
VK573-587	Nautical instruments
VK588-597	Marine hydrography. Hydrographic surveying
VK600-794	Tide and current tables
VK798-997	Sailing directions. Pilot guides
VK1000-1249	Lighthouse service

Navigation. Merchant marine - Continued

VK1250-1299	Shipwrecks and fires
VK1299.5-1299.6	Icebreaking operations
VK1300-1491	Saving of life and property
VK1500-1661	Pilots and pilotage

Subclass VM

VM1-989	Naval architecture. Shipbuilding. Marine engineering
VM15-124	History
VM165-276	Study and teaching
VM295-296	Contracts and specifications
VM298.5-301	Shipbuilding industry. Shipyards
VM311-466	Special types of vessels
VM595-989	Marine engineering
VM975-989	Diving

CLASS Z - BIBLIOGRAPHY. LIBRARY SCIENCE. INFORMATION RESOURCES (GENERAL)

Subclass Z

Z1001-8999	Bibliography
Z1001-1121	General bibliography
Z1001	Introduction to bibliography. Documentation
Z1003-1003.5	Choice of books. Books and reading. Book reviews
Z1004	Biography of bibliographers
Z1011-1017	General bibliographies
Z1019-1033	Special classes of books
	Including prohibited books, rare books, paperbacks, reprints
Z1035-1035.9	Best books
Z1036	Booksellers' general catalogs of modern books
Z1037-1039	Books for special classes of persons, institutions, etc.
Z1040	Databases. Computer files
Z1041-1121	Anonyms and pseudonyms
Z1201-4980	National bibliography
Z1201-1946	America
Z1215-1363	United States
Z1365-1401	Canada. British North America
Z1411-1939	Latin America
Z1975	Eastern Hemisphere
Z2000-2959	Europe
Z3001-3496	Asia
Z3501-3975	Africa
Z4001-4980	Australia. Oceania
Z5051-7999	Subject bibliography
	Subjects arranged in alphabetical sequence
Z8001-8999	Personal bibliography
	Names of individuals arranged in alphabetical sequence

Subclass ZA

ZA3040-5185	Information resources (General)
ZA3150-3159	Information services. Information centers
ZA3201-3250	Information superhighway
ZA4050-4750	Information in specific formats or media
ZA4050-4460	Electronic information resources
ZA4150-4390	Computer network resources
ZA4450-4460	Databases
ZA4550	Motion pictures. Video recordings
ZA4650-4675	Pictures. Photographs
ZA4750	Sound recordings
ZA5050-5185	Information from specific providers
ZA5050-5185	Government information